**TO MY GRANDMOTHER RUTH
AND MY DAUGHTER, BOTH GONE
BUT NOT EVER FORGOTTEN**

Acknowledgments

Writing a book, for me at least, is an easy thing to do. Getting it produced or even looked at in the first place are the more difficult tasks; made all the more difficult by those others whose attitudes and actions would seem to be geared toward preventing publication of anything, particularly a book. Because of those people, I am doubly appreciative to those who not only helped me but had the faith and quiet understanding all along that not only could this book be published, but that *I* would be the one to write it. Words are not enough to express my sincere thanks to the following people:

James Ronald Reed, whose loving support and heroic patience have enriched the quality of my life tenfold, and because of that has helped to make all things possible.

Bonnie Shubert Sgarro, who generously gave far

more than I probably ever deserved.

Amy Topiel Paul, my friend and my attorney, whose steadfast advice saw me calmly through some exciting beginnings.

Richard Curtis, who, for a fleeting moment was my agent; when that moment was gone, his book, *How to Be Your Own Literary Agent*, served me beautifully.

Then there are the editors. Editors often get a bad rap from writers, but I've been blessed with some wonderful ones. Every writer needs a first break, and I owe that to Bobbie Justice, who first ran my organizing pieces in the *Los Angeles Times*. Nationally my first break was graciously extended by Jennifer Johnson, managing editor of *Redbook*, who published my work and even acted as though she thought I was terrific. At Writer's Digest Books, I started with Editor-in-Chief Carol Cartaino, whose vision, honest integrity, and warmth were deciding factors in my selecting Writer's Digest. And finally, I am grateful to freelancer Beth Franks who performed editorial and organizational miracles on nearly every page of this book.

I have always been a little awestruck over the talents of artists. And the talents of those who have contributed the art and graphics that make up the illustrations here are substantial. I am thankful particularly to Carol Strebel, who is responsible for the marvelous illustrations at the beginning of each chapter. And D & R Creative Services in Los Angeles also made some wonderfully significant contributions to this book, as did Shunichi Yamamoto.

Finally, the people in my life who have provided support and managed to keep my spirits up when the going got rough deserve a special mention of thanks. First and foremost is the courageous New York contingent: Sharon Wong Nord, Sue Lowe Betts, Tracey Cotter Miller, Jean Buchalter, and Mary Finlayson. They've all done more than I could ever do for them. In Los Angeles, those who kept me going include Thom Eubank, Shimon Grill, Chuck Falkenstrom and Ron Posner. Their kind words and periodic assistance made a world of difference.

THANK YOU ALL!

How to get organized when you don't have the time

Stephanie Culp

Cincinnati, Ohio

94   93   10

Library of Congress Cataloging in Publication Data

Culp, Stephanie.
  How to get organized when you don't have the time.
  Includes index.
  1. Time management. 2. Organization. I. Title.
HD69.T54C85   1986   650.1   86-15725
ISBN 0-89879-230-4

Book design by Joan Jacobus
Chapter opening illustrations by Carol Strebel
Illustrations on pages 41, 122, 132, 138, 140, 152, 153, 157, 160, and 183 by Shunichi Yamamoto, Great Western Promotions

Contents

Introduction: You Think You're Disorganized?

You say you're disorganized? Or maybe someone you know is disorganized? Not only that, you've never seen anything as bad as your particular disorganized situation (or that of your friend)! Relax. You're not so bad, believe me. As a professional organizer, I've seen it all—and some of it was absolutely beyond belief! There is a Twilight Zone of the disorganized that is truly amazing and, to all appearances, unfixable. But even the worst cases can be fixed. Let me tell you about some of my more memorable clients.

Take the woman who called me in because she'd had it up to her proverbial *here* and threatened to move out unless her husband got his act together and got himself organized. She couldn't stand the clutter and chronic disorder any longer. His clothes and papers were everywhere. You couldn't walk through the den, really, and because of that, she refused to go in there and watch television with him. So I went in and organized, not only the den, but the whole house. Then I spent half a day with them discussing who was responsible for what—taking out the trash, changing the cat litter, that sort of thing. We worked it all out, made up a schedule of chores to do and who was going to do them. One of the woman's biggest objections was her husband's pants—he wore his jeans two days in a row. Drove her crazy. I wasn't sure two days in a row was such a bad thing; he was in the record business, not the construction business, and anyway, when I was a kid my mother made me wear my dress to school two days before it hit the laundry basket. Mothers must be right, right? It turned out the problem wasn't really that he wore them two days straight but that, when he took them off the first day, he dropped them in a heap on the floor, which annoyed her just about to death and didn't do much for the look of the jeans the following day. We finally solved the problem by agreeing that he could wear his pants for two days in a row if he folded them over the back of the chair at night—after all, who among even the most organized of us always hang up our clothes when we take them off? Anyway, why would you *want* to hang up worn clothes with the fresh ones, especially since you are just going to put them back on again in six or eight hours? A little flexibility and common sense saved the day here.

Another client of mine was a therapist as well as an intellectual and a scholar, very well known in certain circles. My first three hours with him were spent talking about his problems. One of them was that his wife was beginning to get a bit hostile and snappish because he was so disorganized that he never had any time for her. (Sound familiar?) And he was seeing so many clients that he never had any time for himself either. Finally we stopped analyzing his personal problems, most of which stemmed from the fact that he never had enough time, and got down to the business at hand, getting him organized, so that he would have a bit more time for everybody.

This man, because of his amazing career and capacities, had papers in rather astounding quantities. But more than that, he had fallen into the three-by-five trap and lay there floundering like a dying fish. The three-by-five trap can best be described as an addiction to index cards. Probably it should be called indexcardosis. This guy was really hooked. On the cards, he wrote insights, addresses, lists, things to do (one thing per card, of course), birthdays, quotations and ideas for his next book, as well as other notes written in shorthand that no one but he could read. He also had an index card system for the books in his library and another for his writings. The real capper was the index card system where he would note, again, sometimes in shorthand, in which drawer certain papers could be found. He needed that because all the papers were so out of order, and in many cases duplicated, that he couldn't find what he needed most of the time. This one index might have worked, except that those particular cards were all mixed up with all of the other cards (are you still with me?), some of which went back as far as 1947. And, of course, he had a follow-up index card system, which made sense in theory, but in reality was mind-boggling. He had *thousands* of cards. His life was somehow intertwined with those cards, and finally everything of a productive nature, particularly where any kind of paperwork was concerned, slowly ground to a halt for him. The first step in getting him organized was to get him off his card habit. Like withdrawal from any addiction, the process was painful for him. But he was, as I say, a brilliant man, and in the end he saw the wisdom of it all and slowly, one card at a time, got rid of the collection. Only then could we proceed to go through all the papers and properly label and file them. I left this man with an organized filing system that included only one index card system to record birthdays and anniversaries. Total withdrawal from his indexcardosis cold turkey seemed unfair, and he was happy with the results that still allowed him *some* index cards.

By far my most memorable client was a woman who lived in a somewhat secluded area. At her house, birds would fly down and take food from your hand, and occasionally a squirrel would trot expectantly indoors looking for food.

When I arrived, there were cartons and piles of things all over the house. You could not get through any one room unimpeded. The garage was something of a forbidden zone—the smell of mildew wafted out every time I opened the door to gaze at the ceiling-high mess inside. "Did you just move in?" I asked. "Oh no," she replied calmly, "I've been here for six months."

I took a crew and we organized her. It was not an easy job. She saved everything—herbs and twigs (for some medicinal purpose), old catalogs, clothes that went back decades, and just about everything else you can possibly think of.

Her bathroom was jam-packed with bottles and jars of potions—ten bottles of the same shampoo and fourteen tubes of toothpaste—and her kitchen was no better. Dozens and dozens of exotic spices and bottle upon bottle of cleaning fluids I had never heard of were within every cabinet. And yet she never had any food. She would invariably send out to a gourmet shop to have her food (already prepared) delivered.

She was an extraordinary perfectionist, even in the middle of this fantastic chaos she had managed to create for herself. She could spend hours polishing a fork and yet drop an egg on the kitchen floor and leave it there for two weeks.

This woman refused to get rid of anything. At the end of each day, she'd put on gloves and go through the garbage to reassure herself that I had not thrown away something important. She even kept her cat's whiskers as they fell off its fuzzy little face. I bagged, tagged, boxed, filed, and in general, organized everything for this incredible woman. We did her entire house in ten days, and when we were finished, the difference was so astonishing that she had a party for her friends so she could show off her newly organized habitat.

And there've been others. I helped a young woman pack up to leave for her first job away from home—she was going from La Jolla, California, to New York City. There were lots of mother-daughter tears on that job. I worked with a woman who was adding 2,000 square feet to her house. (For those of you unfamiliar with renovation and redecoration, 2,000 square feet is tantamount to building another complete house!) I helped a woman organize, at the last minute, a spectacular party for her husband, a very famous sports figure. I didn't go to the party, but I read about it in the papers. I've had wealthy clients who, because they weren't properly organized, had their utilities disconnected. I've worked with small businesses that were started by some genius who thought that all he needed to be successful was a great idea, and maybe his sister-in-law to answer the telephones. I've organized the paperwork on divorce cases, for property transactions, investments, and lawsuits. I've straightened out the bills as well as the personal paperwork for clients. I've organized closets and garages. You name it, and I've probably seen it or come across it at one time or another. I've worked with decorators, therapists, actors, publicists, producers, housewives, musicians, and more.

These are My People. Most of them are creative and brilliant in their own special ways. I've learned a great deal from all of them, and I like to think I've helped them all (they say I have). As strange as some of My People *may* seem to you (on the other hand, they may not seem strange at all, they may sound just like you), the one thing they all had in common was that they didn't have the time to get organized. The haggling couple, the therapist, and the woman who saved cat whiskers—they were, one and all, too busy to effectively tackle the chaos that had built up around them. Although some of these cases may seem extreme to you, I've found that regardless of the exact circumstances, people hire professional organizers such as myself when the chaos has, in their opinion, taken over their lives. They are finding it difficult to function on a daily basis, and catching up on the backlog of disorganization while they try to keep up with their ongoing obligations seems like an insurmountable task. So they call me or some other professional organizer for a quick fix. Businesses often call in organizers because the backlog is choking the life out of them and preventing them from moving forward with expansion plans they might like to implement. A professional can save the business the time it would take to supervise a staff to clean up the old stuff and make sensible way for the new.

This book is for you if you don't want to or can't afford to call a professional organizer. I've taken what I know, mixed it up with what I've learned from My People, and added some common sense and humor. The more people I speak to through my workshops, private consultations, and public-speaking engagements, the more I realize that, in order to get organized, you must first get control of your *time*. After all, there's no point in tackling the office, the closet, kitchen, or garage, if you don't have the time to do it in the first place.

Because organizing your time is the single most important thread that runs through the organization process, the first part of the book is devoted to getting a grip on time. The second part of the book concentrates on specific areas that seem to be the most common organizational trouble spots. These areas are your space—the kitchen, the closets—the housework, the mail and tons of paperwork that can inundate you, your car, and last but not least, the problems of those other disorganized souls you deal with.

I listed the organizing tips in the second half of the book so that you can easily skip from chapter to chapter and pick the tips you personally need. Almost everyone, disorganized or not, will sometimes have organizational problems in at least one of these areas. You may be lucky—perhaps only one particular area is your problem—for example, your paperwork. Maybe your closets are beautiful, and your car runs like a dream. You've got a housekeeper to clean up the house, including the kitchen and the closets, and those areas are just neat as a pin, thank you very much. In that case, save yourself some more time, and skip those sections of this book and flip directly to Chapter 12, "Papernoia," and get to work immediately organizing your piles of papers.

Or you may find that you have problems in each and every one of those areas, and even though you have tried in the past to get organized, there is now so much clutter and confusion in your life that you're totally overwhelmed. If you think about it, I'll bet you'll realize that the real reason for your delay in facing the "Get Organized" project is first and foremost that you simply do not have the time. But as you read this book, you'll find time you didn't know you had because you'll learn how to make time work for *you*. I'm going to show you how to find the time to get organized so that you can start having the time of your life!

Getting organized doesn't have to be drudgery. It can include a little insight and fun. Just remember, while you're getting yourself organized, that others, many far more disorganized than you, have gotten their acts together and lived to tell the tale. They did it. You can too.

Part 1

Organizing Your Time

One

Finding Time

When are you going to get your act together?

When was the last time someone asked you when you were going to "get your act together"? Naturally, they were referring to your habits and probably your habitat. My personal favorite is when people say, with an exasperated groan, "*Why* are you like this?" Which covers just about everything from compulsive neatness to acute slobbism. The comment is always delivered with the intention of creating total paranoia, guilt, and confusion on the part of the dismayed recipient (you).

I know, I know, you're busy. You've got kids, two jobs, social obligations, creative projects in progress, and a constant stream of visitors for whom you have to drop everything. What are you, the miracle worker? Maybe you should split yourself in two so that you can get everything done all at once and make everybody around you hysterically happy. Except that you suspect that even splitting yourself in two wouldn't give you enough time to get it all done.

But try telling that to the people who are standing around scratching their heads while they wonder aloud why you don't get it together. Everyone—your mother-in-law, your best friend, and your employer—seems to take enormous delight in discussing your imperfections. They point out your problems (as if you couldn't figure them out on your own) and then, profoundly, state that they tell you these things "for your own good."

If you are too fat or too thin, leave it to your friends to bring it to your attention. I'm waiting for the day when not only do they bring it to my attention, they go on the diet and visit the gym on my behalf. If you've got strange taste in clothes, if you are a nervous driver, if you are too pessimistic, count on your "friends" to remind you of these shortcomings.

If your problem happens to be disorganization, lucky you, everybody gets into the act. You hear it not only from your friends but your parents, who never give up on the subject; your mother-in-law, who's convinced that your disorganization is the seed of destruction in the marriage; your employer, who loves to imply that you'll be booted out on your keister any day now because you're so disorganized you don't know up from down; your spouse, who constantly threatens that he/she "can't take it any more"; business associates, who are generally on their fourth drink by the time you screech into the restaurant, late again; and your shrink, who, though he or she says very little, gives you the distinct feeling that you really should clean up your act and get your life organized.

This constant flow of criticism, judgment passing, and downright pressure eventually takes its toll. You ultimately decide "on your own" to get organized. The inspiration to pull yourself together and get organized is often helped along by the observation that your personal productivity level is as close to ground zero as it can get, and your creative (not to mention other) potential has become buried in the chaos.

You finally make the decision to *do something*. Congratulations, you've taken that all-important first step. But wait, there's a major glitch in the "I'm gonna get organized" program. You simply don't have the time to enter into such a project right now. You're so overwhelmed already with everything that you have to do that you flop into bed at night exhausted from the day and panicked at the thought of everything you're supposed to get done tomorrow.

Uh oh. You don't have enough time to get organized. Once you've reminded yourself that you don't have enough time to get organized, it's time for me to remind you that you have the same twenty-four hours in each day that everyone else has—and a lot of people pack a whole lot more into their day than you do. How do they do it? More important, *why* do they do it? What motivates people to "get organized" to the point where their twenty-four hours yield so much more than your twenty-four hours? Try on these motivating reasons for size:

- REDUCE STRESS
- INCREASE PRODUCTIVITY
- RETAIN CONTROL
- GAIN PERSPECTIVE
- ADD TIME TO YOUR DAILY LIFE

REDUCE STRESS

Being disorganized adds stress to your life. If you can't find things when you need them, that's stress. If you are frequently late and/or hurried, that's stress. If you don't have enough time to get everything done that needs to be done, that's stress. I could go on, but let's face it, that would only be stressful. Let me ask you this: Do you drive or take a subway? Do you have children? Do you work for someone else, or are you struggling in business for yourself? Do you have a spouse whom you love, of course, but who is far from perfect? If your answer to any of these questions is yes, then obviously you already know the meaning of the word *stress.*

Driving in jaw-clenching traffic or riding in jam-packed subways; dealing with surly children, crabby spouses, and unreasonable bosses; budgeting money—these things often can't be changed. But, *being disorganized is a condition that can be changed, and that means reducing your daily stress.*

INCREASE PRODUCTIVITY

I don't care what you say, if you are disorganized, you aren't as productive as you could be. And, in today's society, that translates directly into *money,* and sometimes, respect from others. Being chronically disorganized on the job may mean that the promotion you've had your eye on goes to someone else who's more organized than you are. It doesn't matter that somehow you always get the work out, not even if it's better than the other person's efforts. Once your boss attaches the label *disorganized* to you, you're also likely to be labeled with the common translations of *disorganized.* These translations include "flake," "dingbat," "slob," "incompetent," and worse. If you care about your appearance and try to dress appropriately for work or social obligations, then you should worry just as much about your surroundings, and how you handle your daily schedule of obligations. Your surroundings, at home and at the office, say a lot about you, as surely as the clothes you wear do. Upward mobility, if that's your aim, is enhanced by an organized, in-control presence and demeanor. A chronically disorganized person is seen with a giant question mark in the eyes of the beholder. To move ahead, you need to *be* ahead in thought and manner. This is nearly impossible if and when everything is such a mess that you can't find anything—from your pantyhose to the report for the board meeting. Organization means increased productivity, and increased productivity can mean just about whatever you want it to mean. Often it means success, pure and simple.

RETAIN CONTROL

Being organized allows you to take control of your *time, space,* and *life.* Total, chronic disorganization only controls *you.* Daily life loses a lot of its charm when the circumstances around you work together to control you. For example, making an important business deal is impossible when you can't find the contracts and pertinent phone numbers. Looking your best at the office or on a date becomes the ultimate challenge when your closet assaults you each morning with a mess that offers up lots of confusion and absolutely nothing to wear. You say you don't have enough time now? Well, disorganization *guarantees* that you will never have enough time to do everything that needs to be done, and once that particular reality sinks in, the temptation to stay in bed forever starts to try to take over each morning. Your life is no longer your own; it somehow belongs to the mess around you. You think you might be ready to check into the local rest home—you've lost all control. Get organized, and you'll be in control again.

GAIN PERSPECTIVE

Being organized actually heightens awareness and changes your perspective for the better. For example, you'll be able to organize things so you have enjoyable time available for yourself, instead of never having time for everything you need or want to do. You will gain insight regarding what it is exactly that you really *want* to do with your life, on a daily basis. If you are disorganized, it's impossible to see where you're going, because you really don't know where you are. Organization puts not only the *now* but the *future* into proper perspective. You will stop living each day with no apparent purpose other than to do what needs to be done, with no time for anything else.

ADD TIME TO YOUR DAILY LIFE

The biggest bonus in being organized is that, whatever you are trying to achieve, you'll have more time to pursue your dreams and goals. Remember that disorganization and time make up a vicious cycle. You may be too disorganized now to find the time to do what needs to be done, but if you don't find time to get organized, it's a sure bet you'll never have enough time for everything else in your life. But if you can get yourself organized, and *stay* organized, you'll find blocks of time available that you never dreamed existed.

Knowing the benefits you receive from getting organized can sometimes help in the motivation department, but really, just exactly *how* are you going to get organized when you really still think you don't have enough time? You *want* to get your act together, you just *can't*. The Problem, you've always told yourself, is finding the *time* to get organized. Of course you'd do it if only you had that always elusive *time* that's required to *actually get organized*. I'm going to remove that one barrier you've had to getting organized—time. I'm going to show you how to have enough time to get organized and *stay* organized. For *your own good*, of course.

And the bottom line is that this *is* all for your own good. As we grow up we are taught many lessons that we initially may resist but, thanks to our mothers (or fathers), we learn, *for our own good*. Dressing oneself, for example. Getting up in time for school. Taking on additional responsibility. It is all for your own good, and you learn it *or else*.

Eventually we make it to adulthood and venture forth on our own. Now who is there to teach us, *for our own good?* If you'll consider the people in your life, you may realize that other people still do things for your own good—your husband, your mother (still!), your mother-in-law (oh boy), and your employer. More often than not, all they do is irritate and annoy you with their "efforts" in your behalf. You know what's good for you; why don't they just butt out? And you know what? You're right. You *do* know what's for your own good, and furthermore, deep down, you probably know that getting organized is in that category.

If you are like most people, you probably overcomplicate your own time-management problems. You think you are different or special. Nobody has quite the demands placed on them that you do. We all like to think that we are more complex than the next person, but the reality is that when it comes to getting the most out of your time, certain aspects of the problem are absolutely universal.

As life-styles become more complicated, organizing the time to accommodate the demands of the average day becomes the ultimate challenge. Losing and forgetting things, being chronically late, never having enough time in the day to get everything done—these are but some of the symptoms that indicate your life could use a general time-management overhaul. In the next few chapters, you'll learn how to manage your time so that you can have organizational control. But before we attack the major barrier, *time,* let's assess your specific organizational hot spots. The following quiz will help you see exactly how organized you are now.

WHAT'S YOUR ORGANIZATION I.Q.?

To find out how Culpable you are, answer the following questions, yes or no.

1. Have you reached the point where you find yourself deliberately not opening the mail for days at a time? (After all, you haven't taken care of yesterday's mail, how on earth can you face today's?)

YES _____ **NO** _____

2. Does the top of your desk look like the national archives? Is it so cluttered with piles of paper that you don't have any space left to do your work?

YES _____ **NO** _____

3. Do you tell everyone around you not to touch a thing on your desk, because in spite of the apparent mess, you know *exactly* where everything is?

YES _____ **NO** _____

4. Has your telephone, electricity, or other utility been turned off, or have your credit cards been stopped, simply because you forgot to pay the bill, and not because you didn't have the money?

YES _____ NO _____

5. Are some of your friends and relatives annoyed because you never have the time to return their calls or answer their letters?

YES _____ NO _____

6. Do you keep piles of newspapers and magazines you haven't read because there's something very important that you *must* read in each paper or magazine? You simply *have* to read it all, but so far, you haven't had the time to do so?

YES _____ NO _____

7. Does your hall closet remind you of Fibber McGee? Did the pots and pans stage an outright revolt the last time you opened your kitchen cupboard?

YES _____ NO _____

8. Do you have piles of things in your house or office—are things stuffed under the bed, stacked in boxes, or packed in bags, all waiting for the day when you have the time to go through everything and then figure where to put it? (You keep telling yourself if only . . . if only I had the time . . . if only I had more closet space . . . if only I had two more filing cabinets . . . if only I had a bigger office. Do you have the "if only's"?)

YES _____ NO _____

9. Is your garage so full of *stuff* that there's no room for the car?

YES _____ NO _____

10. Do you find yourself avoiding phone calls and socializing because you just don't have the time to deal with people, or just don't *feel* like dealing with them?

YES _____ NO _____

11. Do you often have a problem figuring out what clothes to wear even though your closet is full of clothes?

YES _____ NO _____

12. Does your day usually start with a crisis (can't find your keys, nothing to wear, late for work, etc.), and get worse from there?

YES _____ NO _____

13. Do you have a difficult time making decisions, and because of that, often put off making the decision until the situation becomes an emergency?

YES _____ NO _____

14. Are you very particular about how things are done, and how they look? For example, does it concern you if a postage stamp is crooked on your outgoing correspondence, and do you take pains to see that your handwriting is perfect?

YES _____ NO _____

15. Do you have so many "to do" lists that you don't know where to begin?

YES _____ NO _____

16. Do you feel uncomfortable about hiring others to do things for you, since you are certain (based on experience, no doubt) that they will not be able to do the job properly, and because of that, you might as well do it yourself?

YES _____ NO _____

17. Do you have trouble finding enough time for all areas in your life—work, play, family, and spiritual needs, plus some private time for yourself?

YES _____ NO _____

18. Do you forget important dates, such as anniversaries and birthdays?

YES _____ NO _____

19. Do you think that perfectionism is the same as excellence?

YES _____ NO _____

20. Are you constantly plagued by interruptions from others and as a result never seem to get anything done?

YES _____ **NO** _____

21. Have you given up trying to balance your checkbook but at the same time you haven't given it to a professional so that it can be balanced for you?

YES _____ **NO** _____

22. Do you have some kind of legal or accounting problem pending that could have been avoided (be honest!) if you had been more organized? (You didn't pay a parking ticket, your taxes are overdue, someone is taking you to small-claims court.)

YES _____ **NO** _____

23. Do you often want to stay in bed instead of getting up to face yet another chaotic day?

YES _____ **NO** _____

24. Have you missed out on a promotion, a sale, or an opportunity of some kind because you didn't have the time to get organized so that you could make a proper presentation?

YES _____ **NO** _____

25. Do you often find yourself agreeing to do something just because you didn't know how to say no, and as a result you spend an inordinate amount of time trying to get out of the obligation?

YES _____ **NO** _____

26. Is the clutter in your life so overwhelming that you don't know where to begin to sort it all out?

YES _____ **NO** _____

Scoring:

In an effort to keep things simple, and so you don't have to spend a lot of time figuring the mathematics of scoring, simply give yourself one point for each yes.

If Your Score Is

1-6 Congratulations. You seem to be relatively organized. Additional organizational tips in this book can only streamline your already organized manner. You probably have good time management, but again, you may find some useful tips that you hadn't employed before.

7-12 Uh, oh. You've got a little problem with time and/or organization. It's probably time to begin cleaning up your act by implementing the plans outlined in this book.

13-15 If you feel as if you have totally lost control, chances are you have or are about to. Your organizational problems are compounded by your apparent lack of time. Reclaim control over your life by putting yourself on the program outlined in this book.

16-26 You're so disorganized, you probably don't know if you are coming or going. Chaos is probably a way of life for you. And you know what that means. Your life is running you, instead of you running your life. It's time for an organizational overhaul, no question about it! You can begin by following the time-management program set down in this book so that you will then have the time to get organized!

Two

Time Is Money

The cost of disorganization

"The bottom line"—that's a phrase we hear all too often today. "What's the bottom line?" someone will ask (usually impatiently), and suddenly you have to come up with a concise, to-the-point answer. Many times, the bottom line is directly linked to the cost of something, whether it's represented by time expended or actual dollars. I always like to think that the bottom line in getting organized is the cost of disorganization itself. Or, simply put, the bottom line is that *time is money*. So if I still haven't convinced you of the many benefits of organization, why not try on the negatives for size? Do you have any idea exactly how much disorganization is costing you right now? Consider this true story:

A woman from Beverly Hills is driving her BMW merrily along when she makes an illegal turn. Naturally, she gets a ticket from a very alert Beverly Hills policeman. She signs the ticket and drives on. The ticket will cost her about fifty-six dollars. She's not too organized, and she loses the ticket. The next thing you know, she gets a summons to appear in court. She is still not too organized about the whole matter, and at the last minute she hires a very young, very new-in-the-business attorney. This greenhorn accompanies her to court and, once there, advises the woman to plead temporary insanity, which she stupidly does. The court remands the woman to the local women's jail, where she is to be housed while she undergoes a battery of psychiatric tests. After a couple of weeks of this indignity, she is pronounced sane, and released—but not before she pays psychiatric bills totaling thousands of dollars. The court has demanded that she pay up, since she is clearly not indigent. Furthermore, since she has been pronounced sane, she also has to pay the ticket, the lawyer, and the court costs.

I believe the woman went on to sue the greenhorn lawyer for malpractice, and *that* cost buckets of money as well.

Being disorganized can be downright expensive, no question about it. Disorganization can cost you:

A PROMOTION

FRIENDS

MONEY

TIME

and will most certainly result in continued aggravation and stress all around.

THE COST OF *GETTING* ORGANIZED

And what's it going to cost you to *get* organized? You may need to buy a notebook or day planner, proper filing systems, and some gadgets that help keep things organized (such as a shoe rack or a special unit for your records and tapes). Or if you hired people to help you, that would cost money. You can get around the expense of hiring people on this project, of course, if you decide to do it all yourself. What's that you say—you can't afford to hire people, and there's no way you can do it yourself because you don't have enough time? Baloney. On the first point, you probably *could* find the money to hire people if you wanted to. Consider it an investment in your future. You buy clothes to enhance your image; you buy cars and briefcases, you buy, buy, buy, and give yourself all sorts of reasons why you are buy, buy, buying. Actually, most of these purchases are just things that you *want* that don't have much to do with your future at all. Being organized, on the other hand, has everything to do with your future, and then some.

But if you really don't want to hire help, or can't pay for it, then it's up to you to *find* the time to do it. Don't even think that you can't "afford" the time to do it. Because

TIME IS MONEY

and don't you ever forget it. Time is also life—after all, life is made up of time, and when your time runs out, that's it. So, if you understand that time is money, and time is life, you can't help but appreciate the value and consequently the *cost* of your time. Here's how it works:

HOW MUCH ARE YOU WORTH?

We live in a society that places a value on what one does for a living. I'm not saying that this value system is good or bad, I'm just saying it exists. It's probably not always a fair value system, either. The average housewife and mother works plenty hard, but because society hasn't fixed a monetary value on that occupation, her services are often taken for granted and grossly undervalued by those around her—and in fact, often by those she is serving (husband and children). But let's look at that. What services does the wife and mother provide? She probably regularly does the following:

COOK

KEEP HOUSE

BABYSIT (ROUND THE CLOCK)

ENTERTAIN

PROVIDE ERRAND AND TAXI SERVICE

LAUNDER AND IRON

And those are just the bare basics. She has probably decorated the house (with or without money, the wife and mother often turns a house or apartment into a *home*). If she sews, she does the work of a seamstress or tailor and saves money at the same time. Often she's responsible for the family finances and budget and therefore does what a bookkeeper or financial planner might do. Finally, she keeps everything and everybody *organized*. And the wife and mother often works such long hours that you can't easily figure the exact number of hours she puts in per week. She's often the first one up in the morning and the last one to bed at night, and even if she's watching television, more often than not she's mending or ironing—let's face it, she never stops. Good grief. This woman is not only amazing, if you had to pay outside people for all of those services, it would cost a bloody fortune. But by determining what others charge for the services the wife and mother provides without compensation, you can place a value on her time. Experts have placed a yearly value of $15,000-$20,000 on the homemaker's services, but I'm afraid that if I broke the per-year figure into an hourly wage I'd be mortified, and there might be a revolt among homemakers for better working conditions!

Let's examine another situation. Suppose you are a manager of a department in a corporation and you make $35,000 per year plus benefits. This breaks down to $673.08 per week (for a forty-hour week), or $16.83 per hour. So, $16.83 per hour is the cost of your time. Except that, in reality your time is worth even more than that. Because the corporation pays for your insurance and maybe contributes to a pension plan or savings plan in your behalf. If you weren't working at all and had to pay for these benefits yourself, they would cost you a pretty penny. Since benefits can be so varied, for the sake of simplicity let's add $1.00 to the hourly rate of $16.83, and now your time is worth $17.83. Ah, but what about taxes, you ask. What about them? Some people pay, and some people don't, depending on the situation. Since I am not a tax expert and don't know what bracket you are in or how you are handling the matter of taxes, let's, again for the sake of simplicity, deduct that $1.00 we just gave you for benefits. You're back to $16.83 per hour. And now, to keep it really simple, and because our mathematics has been more than a little funny up to now, let's go one step further, and round that number off to $17.00 per hour. There. You, the manager, are worth $17.00 per hour.

That's one way to figure it. The other way is to assume that you're probably not going to get paid what you're *really* worth, all things considered, so you might as well sit down and assess what you're worth based on your own talents, common sense, and value as a human being.

WHERE DOES THE TIME GO?

Once you've figured out—or *decided*—what you're worth, you need to take a look at how you're spending all this valuable time. The most common way to do this is to keep a time log for a week or two. Essentially this involves writing down just about everything you do including brushing your teeth and gabbing on the phone and making a notation regarding how much time you spent doing any one thing. Generally, after keeping a time log for a couple of weeks, it becomes glaringly apparent that you are wasting precious time in several different ways, and that others are adding to the problem by wasting your time (which you allow), and, not only that, you might even see that you are also guilty of wasting others' time. You'll also spot interruptions that could have been avoided or cut short, duplicated efforts, and countless other time-wasting maneuvers on the part of yourself and others. If you've got the discipline to do it, keeping a time log can be a real eye-opener.

Most people find the time log a hard candy to swallow, even though two weeks' worth of it almost invariably shows that you are in the habit of wasting an inordinate amount of time and that that wasted time could easily be turned into *saved* time—time enough to invest in your future by getting organized. If you can't make yourself keep a time log, try buying one of those digital wristwatches that has a built-in beep that sounds when a certain amount of time has elapsed. One of my clients did this: once each hour his watch beeps, and he is jolted back to the reality of how much time he is spending (or wasting) on any given project, person, or day. Beep . . . another hour of your life gone—how did you spend it? Beep . . . how are you going to spend the hour coming up?

Never lose sight of what you're worth per hour. While you are filling your time log with notations like, "Stopped at the cleaners and drug store—1 hour," remember what that hour cost you. Why didn't you hire the kid down the street for a few dollars to do that? Now you'd have your cleaning, the items from the drugstore, and one hour to be used on your "getting organized" project, so that you will have more time to pursue your goal of becoming a vice-president with a corner office and a salary of $45,000 per year, or $21.63 per hour. Or use that time to goof off, if that's what you really want.

And what about your family? You say you never have enough time to spend with your family? Now the cost of time goes beyond money in a really serious way. If your family died in a car crash tomorrow, how would you feel about the time you had already spent with them—that dollars-per-hour time? Any nitwit knows that you can't place a monetary value on human life and relationships, and yet a lot of people don't pay attention to this sad fact until it is too late. If you spend the time it takes to get organized, chances are that not only will you have the time to take the necessary steps to move ahead in your chosen career, but you'll have more time for the important people in your life as well.

For although we can fix a monetary value on each hour, the truth is that time has a value that's immeasurable in human terms. Benjamin Franklin coined the time-is-money phrase, but he also pointed out that "time lost is never found again." Consider that often when we talk of time, we talk of the time we *spent*. You do spend time, and the *way* you spend it, like the way you spend your money, yields certain results and consequences. By getting organized, you'll gain such returns that the time you spend on the project will, in the end, be minimal at best.

Very well, you may say, but how am I going to *find* the extra time to do this—forget what the time is worth in dollars!

The first thing you need to do is to stop saying that you don't have enough time. Look at the time in your life as a positive force rather than a negative one. When someone asks you to do something, instead of automatically checking your calendar to see if you can "fit it in," first ask yourself this:

Do I want to take advantage of this opportunity?

or

Shall I take part in this particular activity?

Now, instead of time management, you are into opportunities or activities management. And once you shift into opportunities or activities management, you automatically make the shift to *life management*.

CHOOSING YOUR OPPORTUNITIES AND ACTIVITIES

And once you decide to manage your life, you have already taken the first all-important step to gaining *positive* control over your time and organizational problems. Life management, as I see it, is a way, not only to solve time and organizational problems, but also to *enhance* the time of our lives. Because each day you wake up is another day that you have been given to do with as you wish. Yes, *as you wish*. You *can* change your life so that you take advantage of activities that you think of as opportunities, and you *can*, if you *want* to, make your life a manageable one. After all, there is no Great Law that decrees that you have to say yes to every activity or demand (or for that matter, "opportunity") that comes your way. You *can,* and no doubt should, say *no* more frequently. It probably won't kill anybody (though when chronic "yes-ers" finally start to say no, you'd think the world was coming to an end). Once you experience the result that your no produces (everybody survives, and you're greatly relieved that you don't have to schedule in that one more thing that you grudgingly agreed to in the first place), you'll find that the act of saying no is one of the most liberating things you can do for yourself in terms of freeing up more time in your life.

Of course, obligations need to be handled, and they are, after all, a part of life. But if you'll stop right now, this minute, and tell yourself that you are entering into a *life management* plan—instead of thinking of it as a *time-management* system loaded down with ugly disciplines that you're sure you'll hate—you'll have a much better chance of success. You can help yourself by asking yourself periodically if you really *want* something (or someone) in your life. Too often we go through life on automatic pilot. We get up, get dressed, and hurl ourselves headlong into the day, without giving any thought to the meaning or the consequences of how we subsequently spend or waste that particular day. We find ourselves agreeing to things without giving the matter careful thought, and before we know it, we're running around like the proverbial chicken without a head. And in the meantime, we're definitely not getting any younger. Life, we become convinced, is passing us by.

And the truth is, life *is* passing you by—and at an alarming speed, too. How can you reverse that out-of-control spiral that seems to be taking over the days of your life?

It's really simple when you use my life-management plan. Remember, it's *your* life. How are *you* going to manage it? You'll begin by making decisions about how to manage your life on a *daily* basis, because life is lived daily, hour by hour, minute by minute. To help you make the daily decisions on how to manage your life more effectively (and, in the process, more pleasantly), train yourself to ask these questions on a regular basis:

Do I really want this in my life?

Is this an opportunity or an unnecessary burden?

Will I or someone else benefit from this?

and so on. In short, are your activities opportunities that you want in your life?

Of course, it's very easy to train yourself to ask yourself the activities/opportunities question before you look at your calendar, but what criteria do you use to figure out the answer? If you automatically go to the calendar to see if you want the opportunity/activity, you're still going about it incorrectly. To make the switch from never having enough time to instead having time to invest in activities and take advantage of opportunities that might enrich your life, you will look at your calendar only at the end of a five-step plan. This plan takes you right up to some extra time for yourself—and that means (if you want it to) you'll have time to get organized.

FIVE-STEP PLAN FOR SUCCESSFUL LIFE MANAGEMENT—AND MORE TIME!

1. MISSION
   Identify your mission in life.

2. GOALS
   Set and prioritize goals to achieve mission.

3. UNFINISHED BUSINESS
   List unfinished business and to dos.

4. PROJECTS
   Transfer to dos to projects list and prioritize.

5. SCHEDULING
   Schedule your plan of attack.

Three

Making Time Work for You

So much has been written about the subject of time management that the very topic has become "overgrown." I've heard of methods so complicated I couldn't see how the average person would ever find the time to figure the system out, much less implement it.

But with my simple (yes, really!) Five-Step Plan to Life Management, you can see results almost immediately—providing you put it to work.

The first step is very important: *identify your mission in life*. I suppose there are other words you could use instead of *mission*—*purpose, objective,* even the word *meaning* could perhaps be used. But *mission* really takes all of those words together and gives them a little push, and a little push is what we all need from time to time. And this time, the enormous meaning of the word *mission* should give you that much-needed push to get started in a serious, meaningful way on the Five-Step Plan.

STEP ONE: MISSION

Take some time right now, at the beginning of this five-step plan, to consider your mission in life. What is it? Is it to help others? To become a success in your chosen field? To raise a family with values that will carry on in your name? Whatever. Come up with a purpose for your life. A short paragraph will do. But do it now. Don't wait until you are a disorganized ninety-five years old. Trust me—it'll be too late then.

Writing down your mission in life can be difficult. It certainly requires some thought. But if you procrastinate on this step, or whine that you simply *can't* do it, or don't know *how* to do it, or ask *why* you should do it—what's it got to do with more time to get organized, anyway?—then you will never get more time to get organized. 'Nuf said. Write down your mission. *Now.*

To help those of you who are stuck, here is an example. Assume, for the duration of this book, that part of your mission is,

**TO ACHIEVE INNER PEACE AND SERENITY;
TO LEAD A SUCCESSFUL AND PRODUCTIVE LIFE
THAT INCLUDES THE ENJOYMENT
OF QUALITY RELATIONSHIPS;
AND TO RECEIVE A DEGREE OF RESPECT
FROM OTHERS.**

If you have trouble coming up with a suitable statement, you might ask yourself what the mission was for:

GOLDA MEIR

JOHN LENNON

JOHN KENNEDY

ABRAHAM LINCOLN

MARTIN LUTHER KING

WINSTON CHURCHILL

ELEANOR ROOSEVELT

FLORENCE NIGHTINGALE

BABE RUTH

LUCILLE BALL

I'd be willing to bet that if you could talk to each of these people they would tell you that they felt a sense of their mission in life—whatever the area—and that this feeling of mission kept them focused and served as a silent guiding light throughout their life.

Remember these people as you consider your mission. Your tendency may be to lay it aside and forget it, since the contemplation of something so serious and personal can often make people uncomfortable. But I cannot overemphasize the importance of this first step. Each step in the five-step plan takes a little time. But once you have taken yourself through each step, you will see that the time you spent in order to gain more time has been well worth it. Each step flows logically into the next step, and as with many things in life, the first step is the most difficult. But this first step—mission—like many valuable first steps, will make a world of difference in how successfully you will be able to handle the following steps.

STEP TWO: GOALS

Oh, I know, this one is too impossible to consider, and what does it have to do with finding the time to get organized, anyway? Just about everything, that's all. And, as with step one, mission, if you balk at doing this one, goals, you are not going to succeed at managing your time.

In order to work toward and hopefully achieve that purpose in your life, I am going to assume that you will need to get organized, since an organized life and thought process can enhance and promote all the components of any mission.

Now it follows that "getting organized" is one of your goals. Try this exercise:

List goals that will help you achieve your mission. List at least two goals that you would like to realize in six months to a year, at least two goals you want to accomplish in five years, and at least two goals you hope to achieve in your lifetime. I'd be willing to bet that "getting and staying organized" (if you are currently disorganized—and if you aren't disorganized, why are you reading this book?) will show up on the six-months-to-a-year list, at the very least, and you assume that once that is achieved you can get on to more exciting goals for five-year and lifetime time frames. And of course you are right. Finding time and getting organized does open the door to the increased availability of options that you can, if you like, turn into goals.

Gee whillikers, looks like you should get organized. It makes some sense, it's a goal, and it fits in with your mission in life. So now when an activity or opportunity presents itself, before you hit the pages of your calendar, ask yourself, Does this fit in with my mission, and therefore, my goals in life?

Remember that your goal is to get organized so that you can work toward your mission in life. As demands are placed on your time, stop long enough to mentally take yourself through this mission-and-goal review, and you'll find gobs of time you never dreamed could be available to you.

But let's go back to your six-months-to-a-year list. You probably wrote down "get organized," and for your second goal, you may have written just about anything from "lose twenty pounds," to "find a new job" or "buy a house." Or you may have written that you want to buy a new Mercedes, and this car will cost you a whopping $40,000. By george, you really *want* that Mercedes, and oh yes, by the way, you currently make in the neighborhood of $22,000 per year. "This is great," you say to yourself. "I can't wait to show off in that baby, and all I have to do is set a goal, write it down, and make a plan. Yeah, sure, I'll get organized, too, but zippety doo dah— we're talking car, right now! Where's the keys to the Mercedes?"

Hold it. Even if I buy your ridiculous rationalizations about how that Mercedes ties in to your mission in life (showing off is a reason)—the fact is, you'll never get the car, because you have put the cart before the horse, so to speak, and now there's no possible way the cart will roll down the road. Get a grip. You will *not* get that car this year, even. However, if you look at that goal a little more closely, break it down, and plan for it, it is possible that you *may* get the Mercedes sometime. Here's what I mean:

First, ask yourself what you need to get that car. The answer, obviously, is first and foremost money. Lots of it. And right now you don't have it. I mean, you can hardly afford to pay the rent, buy food, and catch a movie or two, what with prices as high as they are today. So already you've got a problem with this goal, and the problem is money. Naturally, you are now going to look me straight in the face, sneer, and say, "I told you so. Setting goals is a bunch of you know what."

But, wait, what about your mission in life—you know, the peace and serenity, productive success, and respect from others—all that stuff? Just because you *want* the car to show off in, that doesn't tie in to your mission and you know it!

Uh, well (you're ready to let me have it now) a Mercedes commands respect and looks successful, and if you look successful, it actually helps you become successful. After all, you gotta spend money to make money. . . .

What about peace and serenity . . .?

You've got to be joking! Have you ever taken a spin in a Mercedes? I mean, talk about smooth . . . we're talking totally serene!

Whoa, slow down now. I didn't say you couldn't get the car. I merely said you couldn't get the *new* Mercedes car, now, this very instant. Ask yourself a couple of things. First, ask yourself what, if any, other options you might be willing to consider. For example, you might want to think about a used Mercedes rather than a brand new one. If you are willing to adjust your expectations to realistic levels, your goals will become more manageable. In that case, you might realistically expect to be able to buy a used Mercedes, in excellent condition, within twenty-four months. During that twenty-four-month period you'll have to pursue certain systematic steps in order to realize your goal—ownership of that Mercedes.

So to begin with, get that Mercedes goal off the six-month page and put it on the two-year-goal page. It is simply not going to happen in six months. You *might* make it in two years, if you consider the following:

Not only will you need to save money, you will probably need to figure out a way to make a little more money. Perhaps you could take freelance or part-time work in addition to the job you already have. Maybe you can trim your spending so that you can save a bit more from your current budget. Remember, you are working toward a *goal*. Maybe you need to clean up your credit rating so that if you buy from a dealer you can finance the car without a problem. You may need to apply yourself a bit more at your job, go after that promotion which, if you really tried, you could have in twenty-four months. Think about it all. Chart the steps that will be required to achieve your goal, and then work methodically toward that goal by following the steps you have set for yourself. As you succeed in gaining more time for yourself, you will see more specifically how to plot and plan and schedule the time necessary in pursuit of goals. Just know for now that you should begin by setting small goals and deadlines within the major stated goal. For example, tell yourself that you are going to find an additional part-time job no later than four weeks from now, and then set that date with yourself by writing that deadline down. Then *do* it!

Remember that setting goals, and planning for those goals, with realistic expectations in mind, is what makes good things happen. Suppose at the end of twenty-four months you are still short by $5,000 for the used Mercedes? You don't have the Mercedes, but perhaps you do have a promotion, a good credit rating, and a healthy start on a substantial savings account. Things could certainly be worse. Maybe at the end of the twenty-four months you will extend your "buy the Mercedes" deadline another twelve months, or maybe you will decide to use the money and your credit rating and new status at work to invest in some property somewhere. Did the goals you set and the plans you followed over the last twenty-four months hurt you? Not really—you actually are sitting pretty. What would have happened if you had waited and not planned anything or set any goals whatsoever? You would probably be broke because you didn't save any extra money; disgusted with your job because it hadn't changed at all, and, to top it all off, you'd still be driving that old rattletrap you've driven for the past eight years because, would you believe it, in the last twenty-four months, a Mercedes did *not* fall out of the sky and land, with a happy thunk, in your driveway.

And that, in a nutshell, is how goal setting works. Suppose you reach the age of fifty and find yourself hopelessly lost in a severe depression because the truth is, you always wanted to obtain a college degree, and now you're fifty and it's too late. It is *not* too late, it is *never* too late. Go back to school. Go nights. (You'll find the money.) So it will take ten years. So what? What else will you be doing when you are sixty years old? I'll tell you what you'll be doing if you don't get your behind back in school—you'll still be whining that you wish you had gone to college to get your degree.

Not only will goal setting help you with your getting-organized project, but you'll soon be amazed at the practical daily application of this mission/goal process in your life. Take the day I received a sale catalog from Saks Fifth Avenue. I like Saks, I can't afford to go there really, but I think it is a great store. I even have a credit card there. Well, in this particular catalog they had a fabulous black suit *on sale*. It was the right color, fabric, cut, you name it. It looked terrific, and the price was definitely right. My natural inclination would have been to check the calendar, find a free spot on it, and write down, "go to Saks, try on and buy suit," and then I'd do just that. But I never got as far as the calendar.

The reason I never got as far as the calendar is because I asked myself if that particular black suit, on sale at Saks Fifth Avenue, was going to fit in with my goals, not to mention my mission in life. Sadly, I had to admit to myself that it did not. Where in my mission statement, and my goal list, did I talk about black suits on sale? Not only that, but I honestly had to admit that I already had more clothes than I needed and less money than I *always* need. In fact, one of my goals was labeled "Money Plan." My money plan called for reduced spending and more saving. Not only was this suit not listed in my mission or goal sheet, but it went absolutely contrary to my money plan goal. With a flourish, I threw the catalog away. I achieved the following:

- I SAVED MONEY BY NOT SPENDING IT IN THE FIRST PLACE.

- I KEPT TO MY GOAL (MY MONEY PLAN, WHICH I HAD WRITTEN DOWN).

- I SAVED *TIME* BECAUSE IT WOULD HAVE TAKEN PLENTY OF TIME TO DRIVE TO THE STORE, TRY ON THE SUIT, BUY IT, AND RETURN HOME.

The Mercedes, the college degree, and that fabulous black suit made for a nice little digression. But those things are really all about the same thing—*deciding to make the time to do what you want and need to do to make your life what you want it to be.* And for now, you want your life to be organized. So, whatever else you have written down, write down your *goal* of

GETTING AND STAYING ORGANIZED

and yes, you do have to *write it down.* Goals must be several things. They must be realistic and attainable (Are you willing to make the necessary sacrifice?), and they must have a deadline. And you'd better write down all this information, because studies show that the success rate for people who write down their goals is about ninety times greater than for those who don't. So, if you don't write it down, obviously your chances of ever realizing that goal are reduced considerably.

So now that you're into all of this writing, hop on down to the dimestore or the stationery store and get yourself a three-ring binder, some dividers, and some lined paper to go in the binder.

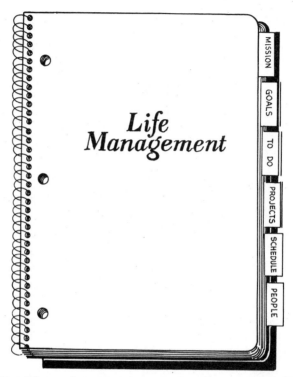

The Five-Step Plan as it appears in your planning notebook. If you're using a loose-leaf binder, you might want to move the "to do" section to the front of the notebook for easier access when you start using your plan on a regular basis.

In the front of your notebook, write your mission statement. You might like to put that on a label and paste it on the cover or on the inside of the cover—that way you'll always be reminded of it.

Then make a section for goals. Write down your goals, one to a page, and give each a realistic (written) deadline.

Now, this notebook is going to help you organize your time so that you'll have the time to get organized. On one of your goal pages, write "Get Organized." Set the deadline at six

PRIORITY

DATE ESTABLISHED

GOAL

DEADLINE

I WANT _____

NO LATER THAN: _____

BECAUSE:_____
(Benefit)

THIS IS ☐ REALISTIC and ☐ ACHIEVEABLE, and ☐ I AM WILLING TO MAKE THE NECESSARY
SACRIFICE

STEPS/TO DO

_____ _____
_____ _____
_____ _____
_____ _____
_____ _____
_____ _____
_____ _____
_____ _____
_____ _____
_____ _____
_____ _____
_____ _____

REMEMBER YOU CAN MAKE YOUR DREAM TRUE WHEN YOU TURN IT INTO A GOAL.

months from now. That's more than enough time. I know this because I have never had a job, regardless of how phenomenal the chaos, that took more than fourteen consecutive days to complete. This means that if I can do it in fourteen days or less, you can do it in six months, no sweat. Not only that, if you use your vacation time to invest in your goal of getting organized (so that you can work toward your life's mission of inner peace and serenity, success and a high level of productivity, quality relationships, and respect from others) you can probably also do the whole thing in two weeks' time.

You've set some goals, including the goal of getting organized, and now you're ready to prioritize your goals. That's easy enough. Here's what you do:

Give each goal a priority number at the top of the page. Remember that goals are goals, not projects or "to do" items. In this case, your goal is to get organized, and we're going to give it a Priority One, because after you get organized, chances are it will be easier for you to logically pursue your other goals in life—which could be just about anything from starting your own business to finding a mate. After all, a business demands organization, and not too many potential mates are turned on by disorganization, which they tend to call slobbism (or worse).

Congratulations. You have now advanced to the third step in the plan. You are almost halfway there. You are just too wonderful for words—give yourself a hefty pat on the back.

Now start a new section in your notebook called To Do, or Unfinished Business. Here comes the fun part.

Four

So Much to Do, So Little Time

Getting a grip on priorities

There are three more steps to go in the five-step plan. When you finish them all you will have made huge progress toward setting your own priorities for the path *you* want to take.

STEP THREE: UNFINISHED BUSINESS

This one is a doozy. Sit down and make a list of all of your unfinished business. This includes pick up the dry cleaning, clean out the closets, organize the car, make up with mother-in-law, finish report for work, call the travel agent—in short, *everything.* Write it all down, even if it's more than a hundred items. All that "to do" stuff swimming in your overwhelmed, disorganized, noggin gets emptied onto the pages in this section of your notebook.

If you are like most people, there are about a zillion

items on the page or pages, and come to think of it, that's exactly why you don't have enough time to get organized. Just *look* at this list! You're convinced you'd have to be superhuman to do all of that and get organized as well!

Well, actually, that's probably true, sort of, but then again, not really. Let me repeat myself—sort of, but then again, not really. Because, would you believe it, you can now start another section in your notebook. You have now advanced another step to more time in your life.

STEP FOUR: PROJECTS

The project section of your notebook is where everything begins to fall together in some semblance of order. This is where you really get organized to get organized.

Begin by taking that enormous list of unfinished business and, one item at a time, transferring it to a project page. Here's how it's done:

Anything that is much more complicated than "pick up the dry cleaning" or "go to the market" becomes a project. For example you may have had "buy that Mercedes" on your list of goals and therefore your list of unfinished business. Purchasing a Mercedes is a project. Make a project page for it. Or perhaps you have been neglecting your relationships. You are remiss in personal correspondence and phone calls, and you owe an apology or two to some people. Make a project page for "Relationships." Maybe you want to go back to school, but you have to research the matter, get money, find the time, etc. Make a page for "Back to School." As you look at your unfinished business list, categories for the project pages will reveal themselves. You will begin to see that a lot of your unfinished business, which you may have thought of as simply things to do, falls into one particular category or a few categories. Some common ones are health, self-development, relationships, career, and money. Use these categories to head up your project pages. Next, transfer everything from the unfinished business list to the project pages.

Of course, since you are going to get organized, that's

definitely a project, so make a project page for "Getting Organized." Everything that has to do with getting organized comes off the unfinished business list, and goes onto the "Getting Organized" project page.

Inertia tends to creep in when you start to think about all the things that need to be done in order to accomplish the "Getting Organized" Project. Your head begins to buzz with what seems like an overload of "to dos," panic sets in, and before you know it, you're ready to throw in the towel before you even start.

Stop!

Remain calm. Just keep writing all of the "to dos" that are currently swimming around in your head on the proper project page. This is how you can instantly get rid of the clutter in your head. As soon as you get it out of there and onto the paper where it rightfully belongs, you'll see that there is not too much after all, and that, with a minimum amount of applied intelligence and attention, you can, in fact, get organized.

By the time you have finished sorting out and transferring your unfinished business to your project pages, you will have noticed (unless you have expired from the experience of actually seeing your unfinished business on paper) that you no longer have a humongous list of unfinished business or "things to do." What you *do* have is several projects with a list of things to do for each project, along with a few leftover things to do, such as pick up the dry cleaning or go to the market.

In the future, when a random "to do" thought pops into your head, get in the habit of immediately jotting it on your unfinished business page. Then, once a day, review that section and transfer any unfinished business that is part of a project onto the proper project page. If it isn't a project, but some maintenance task such as going to the market or the bookstore, schedule it on your calendar. (Hang on, we'll get to that part, scheduling, in the next chapter.)

Now take a look at your project pages, and while you're at it, bear in mind that you should only have three or four projects going at any one time, *tops*. You may have more than that to start with, because things have been so disorganized and haphazard in the past, but now you are getting organized, and once you accomplish that, remember that a couple of projects, in addition to your daily life, are plenty. Be sure to finish one project before you take on any more. This system will help you make quick decisions regarding the time in your life. Now, not only can you ask yourself if the activity, opportunity, or demand being placed on your time fits in with your purpose and goals in life, you can also ask yourself if it's a project, because if it is, and if you already have four projects going, the matter is instantly resolved with a big "No thank you, I can't take that project on right now—I already have *four* projects I'm working on!" And since you should always finish what you start, if you feel strongly enough about something to give it project consideration, then it's worth starting, doing, and more importantly, finishing. The payoff is that the project, once completed, helps you reach your goals and is a part of your overall purpose in life. If you can't see the payoff in those terms, then, quite simply, it doesn't deserve to have the time that a project will require from your life.

To make sure that you don't lose sight of this payoff policy, at the top of each project page that you start, write the *purpose for the project*. Then, as with your goals, give each project a *deadline*. Don't forget that you need to be realistic. Goals and projects are not meant to be dream or wish lists although it has been said that a goal is nothing but a "dream with a deadline." Separate fact from fantasy by understanding that you can realize your dreams if your expectations are in line with reality.

Following your project purpose and deadline, make a notation indicating the *results* you expect upon completion of this project. Now you have finished the thought process that leads to the *reason* to allow that project into your life in the first place.

Let's take our project "Getting Organized":

PROJECT

_____
Date Established

PRIORITY
_____

_____
Deadline

TO DO:_____

NO LATER THAN: _____

BECAUSE:_____
(Benefit)

☐ I PROMISE MYSELF TO WORK ON THIS PROJECT IN AN ORGANIZED MANNER UNTIL IT IS
   F I N I S H E D
☐ I WILL NOT TAKE ON MORE THAN FIVE PROJECTS AT ANY ONE TIME

STEPS/TO DO

_____   _____
_____   _____
_____   _____
_____   _____
_____   _____

NOTES: _____

_____
_____
_____
_____
_____

REMEMBER TO CROSS OFF THOSE STEPS THAT YOU HAVE COMPLETED.

PROJECT   GETTING ORGANIZED

PURPOSE   *So that I can relieve myself of some of the daily stress that plagues me and therefore achieve more peace and serenity. Also so that I can be more productive and successful in my career and personal life and gain respect from others who may not respect me due to my poor organizational habits.*

DEADLINE: *Six months from now*
(write appropriate date)

RESULTS: *Same as "Purpose"*

Make those headings on each of your project pages and fill them in before you do anything else on the project. If you can't fill in those elements of the project, chances are you can scrap it altogether.

Next, do a brief outline of the project. On your "Getting Organized" project page, write the following:

OUTLINE: *Organize the house, including the closets, the kitchen, and the garage. Organize all my paperwork. Most important, organize the way I spend my time (such as with the housework) so that I can have* more *time, and, once organized,* stay *organized, by implementing and living by simple organizational principles that work for me and my environment.*

There's your outline. It's brief, to the point, and just about says it all.

Now that you have licked the mission, goal, unfinished business, and project concepts that will lead to more time in your life (so you can get organized), reward yourself with a treat of your choice, because now, you lucky devil, you're ready to set your priorities.

STEP FIVE: PROJECT PRIORITIZATION

This is pretty simple. Don't let the fact that a few numbers are involved throw you. This is not math, it isn't even close.

First, take each project and give it a priority number. If you have four projects (one of which is to get organized), one project will be a number-one priority, another will be a number-two priority, next will be a number-three priority, and finally, one will be at the bottom of your priorities with a number-four priority. As I said, simple.

Establishing the priority is determined by the purpose for the project, the expected results that the completed project will bring you, and finally, the deadline.

Here's an example of how this works. (You'll probably be thrilled to hear this, since I very nearly botched my plans—but good.) I was working on three projects: (1) to furnish my new office, (2) to prepare for a trip to New York on October 15, and (3) to get material to the publisher by a November 1 deadline. I gave project number one (furnish my office) a January 1 deadline. Now, by looking at the deadlines, I found the priority numbers easy to determine. Preparing for the New York trip became the number-one priority, writing and submitting required material to the publisher became my number-two priority, and furnishing my office was at the bottom of the list of priorities. Thus, the deadlines greatly influenced the priorities, and except for furnishing the office, the deadlines were fixed and could not be changed. The purpose for each project was about the same—they were all business related. In terms of business, submitting material to the publisher was probably the most important, but the New York trip was very, very, close in importance, since I planned to make some far-reaching business deals there. The office needed to be furnished at least minimally so that people would have a place to sit and I would have a place to work. Ideally, of course, I wanted it to be pleasant and somehow impressively wonderful, though I didn't have a clue as to how I was going to pull off that little decorating trick. The expected results also were business related for all three projects—to get and handle *more* business.

The trip to New York required a great deal of advance preparation. The material due the publisher involved a significant amount of work, and furnishing the office seemed to be an endless process, involving decisions and trips here and there to look at, worry over, and buy everything from chairs to picture frames.

I had clearly outlined everything with priority numbers and specific deadlines, but in spite of this, I got caught up in, you guessed it, furnishing my office and somehow let preparations for New York and the work for the publisher go untended for weeks. Suddenly one day, I looked at my project pages and realized with horror that because of the deadlines and the importance of both the trip and the material for the publisher, I had to drop everything, right then, and work on nothing else but those two projects—simultaneously! Now I was in a panic situation, since clearly, if I left for New York on October 15 for two weeks, and the material was due the publisher on November 1, not only did I have to get everything (correspondence, plane tickets, hotel, etc.) arranged and in the mail for the New York trip *at once,* I also had to sit down and do the work for the publisher, since when I returned from New York there would be no time left to work on that project—it would already be November 1, the publisher's deadline.

That is how the purpose and expected results on each project, along with the deadline, will help you decide the priority system. It's a process that almost works by itself. Oh yes, I moved my "Furnish the Office" deadline back; it was March before I finished it. I realized I had allowed myself to get too caught up in that project, probably because I was avoiding the work involved in the other, more important ones.

If you find yourself dwelling on one particular project as I did with the decorating (so you won't have to do the other, more difficult ones), you might want to pull back from that involvement until you make some significant progress on your other projects. Then you can go back to the fun project as a reward to yourself for getting so much done on the others. Deep down, if you are honest with yourself, you *know* which project is the most important and therefore should have top priority. Unfortunately this often seems to be the most tedious project of all. I don't know why this is, but it is good to remember that gratification, alas, is not always instant—and so it goes with projects. Some of the best-laid plans are worked on diligently well in advance of the actual payoff. Don't let that stop you, however. Simply deal with the difficult project regularly (so you can meet the deadline with ease) and advance the easier, more fun project a bit here and there as a reward to yourself for being so good about the other projects, which are, as we both already know, *for your own good.*

Looking Out for Number One

Next, put the priority number at the top of each project page, and then do the organized thing: put the pages in priority order in your notebook, with the most important project first in that section.

Finally, use the same process to prioritize each "to do" that you have listed for your projects (treat each project separately, starting over with number one). Some thought, and often some changing around, will be necessary to get it organized honestly in order of priority.

For example, I once had a writer client who couldn't even work in her office because she could barely get into the room, and when she did, there was no way to locate any of the research information or files that she needed without a thirty-minute search. She had let the papers in her office go untended for years, and now she had deadlines she couldn't meet because she couldn't function there. When I arranged her "Getting Organized" project page, I felt that organizing her office should be high on the priority list—certainly higher than picking out a new bedspread, which was also on that page. But my client refused to be honest with me and, more important, with herself regarding her priorities. She insisted that organizing her office was *not* as important as cleaning out and organizing her seven-year-old daughter's closet. Her defense for this absurd thinking was that she could do the daughter's closet in half a day and therefore she would feel good, whereas doing her office would take much longer and so was harder to deal with and therefore not a high priority.

I can't force you to be honest with yourself; I can only

ask that you approach getting organized with some soul-searching and downright straight thinking. And if your next seemingly unanswerable question is where to begin, do the *worst first*. If you have one especially bad trouble spot, that's where you should begin. If it's all one big series of messes, spilling over into the different areas, then you should probably begin with your overall space. You may want to break your project page "Getting Organized" into segments at this point. For example, one segment might be headed "Organize the Bedroom" (this would include closets, bureaus, and under the bed as well as making any necessary new purchases), and another might say "Organize Paperwork" (this would include the paper in the files, in and on the desk, in the boxes on the floor, and in the shopping bags in the closet). If you do this you will have a separate plan for each area that you tackle, thus breaking the job into smaller, more manageable pieces, which, when put together, equal one big, overwhelming organizing job.

This is the divide-and-conquer approach. Be careful, however. If you use this method, be sure that you do *not* stop after you have done only one area of a total job that includes several areas (or project pages). If you do just a little bit and then drop the project for a while, you will find that the area you organized starts quickly to become overgrown and infested with things from the unorganized areas. You'll find it's best to map out consecutive weekends or days, and not stop until the entire organizing project is completed. (We'll cover scheduling in the next chapter.)

Do the worst first. The rest of the job is much easier to take when you don't have the most dreaded chores still ahead of you.

Now that you have prioritized everything, your "Getting Organized" project "to dos" should look something like this:

TO DO

Find the Time to Get Organized

Keep a time log.

Follow the five step plan.

Get an appointment book to schedule my time to get organized.

Living Room

Need more shelves for books—they're always piled on the floor. Get rid of some?

Have the drapes cleaned, and the rug shampooed.

Get rid of that hideous pillow.

Recover that chair the cats clawed beyond recognition (or replace it).

Rearrange the furniture.

Find the best spot for the stereo.

Buy some plants.

Closets

Hall closet full of junk—sports equipment, board games, crafts supplies, boxes of who-knows-what.

Clean out my closet, get rid of some clothes.

Organize linen closet so everything isn't so crammed in there.

Help the kids organize their closets.

Kitchen

Organize and clean the cabinets.

Hang up some pots and pans.

Get rid of all those empty margarine tubs!

Do I really need 22 knives?

Start planning menus, cooking meals ahead, and freezing them.

What to do about my recipe collection?
Buy a coffee maker with an automatic timer.

Paperwork
Clean out, review, and organize the files.
Buy necessary office supplies: file folders, labels, new in/out baskets.
Make a place to file tax-deductible receipts.
Balance checkbook.
Buy another filing cabinet?
Keep a notebook in the car to write down mileage.

Car
Catch up on car repairs—set up maintenance schedule in mileage notebook and stick to it!
Buy new wiper blades.
Use touch-up paint on the rust spots.
Clean the interior!
Take the box of newspapers I've been storing in the trunk for the past three months to the recycling center.

Here, obviously the number-one priority on the "to do" list of the "Get Organized" project is to find the time to do the project in the first place. If you have followed the first four steps in the plan, you have already seen that you have more time than you thought you did, simply because you've achieved a sense of clarity and direction regarding how you spend your time and, more important, how you *wish* to spend your time in the future. This clarity and direction should make a significant difference in your life from this point forward.

Now some of you are quite ready to advance to the last step in the plan, scheduling. I appreciate such enthusiasm, but I also know that some of you who have come this far, having painstakingly figured out your mission, goals, projects, and priorities, still harbor more than a few doubts about finding the time to get organized.

This uncertainty can generally be traced to some hidden reluctance to get organized in the first place, even though one's purpose and goals really depend on doing so. If this sounds like you or someone you know, the only thing that can be said here is that the reason that the "Getting Organized" project isn't getting done (that is to say, organized) and probably will *never* get done is that the perpetrator doesn't *want* to get it done.

If you (or someone you know) really doesn't want to get organized, and you actually *like* the mess you're in, I could almost bet that you *won't* get organized, no matter what I do or say. I could give you time, tips, and motivation till the cows come home. You're just not interested. But if this is not you, and you really *want* to make a change for the better in your life, you *can* get organized, and, if you are really determined, you can do it by yourself.

Remember that I said from the outset that your deadline for this project was six months. If you really want to badly enough, you can get organized in fourteen consecutive days. Those fourteen days are there, if you want them, in your vacation. Your decision is merely a matter of priorities: which is more important, your vacation or getting organized? Will you really enjoy your vacation, or are you using that vacation to run away from the stress you inflict on yourself through poor organizational habits? Perhaps taking this one vacation to get organized would make future vacations more enjoyable because you wouldn't be so stressed out that you'd need three or four days just to wind down from your normal chaotic state of mind.

If you don't want to take vacation time, or just don't have it available, then you must turn to your schedule to find additional time.

Five

Schedule a Plan, Plan a Schedule

Planning. Now there's a thought. Too often people have a problem with sitting down and making plans, whether for a day, a week, a month, or longer. There are excuses galore that one can use to avoid planning, and I've heard them all. My favorite is, "I like to be spontaneous."

"Planning just isn't my style," the hopelessly disorganized dolt will proudly announce. "People who plan are just too stuffy for me."

Well, listen up, you spontaneous free spirits. Spontaneous is great for a seven year old. It doesn't, however, work terribly well for an adult. So stop making those flimsy excuses and learn to *Run your life instead of letting it run you!* People don't plan to be failures. But they do plan success. Rarely does success just "happen." Famous people interviewed on television or for magazines frequently say that they wanted to be famous or successful even as children, and many of them started planning that success at a very early age. A child going to the movies and dreaming about being a movie star, and then following that dream by establishing goals and eventually *becoming* that movie star, is reaping the benefits of planning. Conversely, the person who never plans beyond a day or two is quite often the victim of poor planning, or to put it another way, *no* planning.

Planning is many things. It is a skill that requires discipline. It is also a habit. Studies show that if you change a habit, or begin a new habit, stick to that change for twenty-one days, you will have made that new change or habit a permanent change or habit in your life. For example, suppose you decide to change your diet. If you can make the change for three weeks, it's a good bet that you will have changed over to that new habit for good.

Take it one bad habit at a time, however. Don't try to renovate your entire life and simultaneously cure all your bad habits, dietary or otherwise, at once. If you do that, you'll only guarantee failure for yourself. That's an example of an unrealistic goal. Trying to change everything, all at once, immediately, is expecting too much of yourself (or anyone else). Make a plan, and take it a methodical step at a time. Your success rate will be much higher.

Beginning the process of planning and scheduling works in much the same way. If you schedule a plan and plan a schedule for three weeks, and stick to both the plan and the schedule for those three weeks, in all likelihood you will have changed your habits enough so that you will then automatically want to plan for yourself on a weekly and a daily basis, thus making your life more organized. At the same time, not only will you be increasing your chances of success and reducing your chances of failure, but you will find yourself more capable of making the time you have count for you.

In a sense, you have already scheduled your plan by stating your mission, defining your goals, and listing your projects. Now it's time to plan more specifically for the achievement of those goals by scheduling your plan of attack. In this particular instance you're going to zero in on getting organized. But this planning process will help you achieve goals and save time in any area—and if you consistently use it as a basis for your pursuit of your purpose and goals in life, you will achieve a measure of success (within reason—remember the Mercedes) that you had not realized could be possible.

IT'S IN THE BOOK

Now you're going to chart your organizational course, to sit down and formulate your plan of attack. Start with a good appointment book that you can work with. If you don't have one, make a section in your notebook under "Schedule," and make it functional by having some sort of monthly at-a-glance calendar (you could probably paste in a page from a wall calendar), a weekly section, and a daily section. You can make your own weekly section by opening a center page and running the week across two pages. The Week-at-a-Glance calendar books in the stationery stores are perfect examples of this format. For the daily section, you will want at least one full page for each day; the Day-at-a-Glance daily planners follow this format, and it works well. Separate your "Schedule" section in your notebook with divider sheets, then, that say "Monthly," "Weekly," and "Daily." Now at a touch, you can turn to the necessary section.

Monthly.　This section is generally used only to make notes of major items, such as trips, birthdays, anniversaries, or holidays.

Weekly.　This section is important and should be filled out at least three weeks in advance. It gives you an all-important overview of your schedule and helps you make wise decisions regarding future commitments.

Daily.　Here is where you itemize all the "to do" things

that you will accomplish that day. Take care to leave some un-booked time on your weekly and dailies. You need some flexibility to accommodate last-minute changes and delays and to break the habit of crisis time management—that is, dropping everything and everybody for the latest crisis that requires your time, and then trying to go back and still do what you originally planned (generally not possible). The daily sheets will get filled up in advance, just as the weeklies are filled up (planned) in advance.

If you are using your notebook, you can follow the style of the Day-at-a-Glance, or you can consider the daily activities sheet from the systems shown on the opposite page. These daily sheets take you step by step through your day, remind you of your goals and projects, and give you plenty of room to list your appointments, "to dos," and calls. They even remind you to review what you accomplished during the day and to transfer what did not get done.

Another good planning system is the Dayrunner. It also provides sections for goals, projects, and scheduling. Dayrunner, like most planners, is subject to constant updating with new forms and ideas, so it always pays to see what they have in the way of planners and forms. It can't hurt to stop by a good office supply store or specialty store to take a look at all of the planners and forms available, if for no other reason than to give yourself some creative ideas about how to customize your own planning system.

Found in specialty stores, the British system, the Filo-fax, is a beautiful and expensive book that also serves as an all-inclusive planning system. Its size appeals to people who prefer something smaller, and its design is the last word in elegance for many.

One of the best overall systems is the Day-Timer system. When you order from Day-Timer, you can pick your own size and format, thus designing your own time manage-

DAILY ACTIVITIES

Day/Date _____

THOUGHT FOR THE DAY _____

TODAY'S PRIORITY _____

DO _____

CALL

No. 160

SCHEDULE YOUR DAY

Today's Actions Determine Tomorrow's Results

☐ Review Goals ☐ Select Items To Do ☐ Visualize Day's Results
☐ Transfer Appointments ☐ Review Other
☐ Select Project Items ☐ Prioritize Daily Activities ☐ Review Finances

THIS WEEK'S GOAL _____

SCHEDULE

	3:00
	3:
8:00	4:00
8:	4:
9:00	5:00
9:	5:
10:00	6:00
10:	6:
11:00	7:00
11:	7:
12:00	8:00
12:	8:
1:00	
1:	
2:00	
2:	

COMPLETE THE DAY

☐ Identify Any Incomplete Items And Transfer
☐ Acknowledge Results Produced Today
☐ Schedule Tomorrow

TODAY'S NOTES _____

No. 160

© 1980 Lee Berglund

Created and designed by Lee Berglund

ment system to suit your particular needs. Besides planning systems, they offer a selection of additional systems you can set up, including, for example, a Family Record & Inventory binder which will accommodate all pertinent information concerning your family's personal and financial records.

These books are more than appointment books or calendar books—they are total planning systems that incorporate your goals into your daily activities and opportunities management—time management, remember? To give you an idea of the possibilities with these books, you can buy sections entitled "Memory," "Fitness Planner" (handy for those people whose goal is to lose weight or gain muscles), "Resource Network System" (for listing special resources that you might use), "Notes," "Goals," "Projects," "Communication Log" or "Agenda," "Guest List," and "Prospects List." You can also find inserts to help you keep records on your finances, your car mileage (now necessary in some cases for the IRS), your check register and check-deposit record, your expenses, and even, believe it or not, items loaned or borrowed.

Sounds mind-boggling, doesn't it? In a way it is, but in another way, systems like the Day-Timer, Dayrunner, and Filofax are exciting in that they let you pick and choose what you need in order to track your goals and schedule your time to pursue your overall plans. These books certainly let you schedule your plan and plan your schedule. You can carry them with you to record things as they happen or occur to you —thus eliminating the clutter in your head as it occurs, immediately, and still not losing the thought. These books provide totally self-contained goal- and time-management systems. If you really use one, it will be very nearly impossible for you to lose sight of your goals, plans, and schedule. You'll find more information on these planning books in Appendix A.

Essentially, you can work from your notebook, and a Week-at-a-Glance calendar book, or you can take your mission, goals, projects, and scheduling and transfer them to a system like the Dayrunner or Filofax, which promise to organize your time so that you have time to stay organized.

WEEK
JAN FEB MAR APR MAY JUN
JUL AUG SEPT OCT NOV DEC
Circle each month

THINGS TO DO TODAY ™

WEEK ENDING

MONDAY DATE	TUESDAY DATE	WEDNESDAY DATE	THURSDAY DATE	FRIDAY DATE	SATURDAY DATE

AM
7:00
7:
8:00
8:
9:00
9:
10:00
10:
11:00
11:
PM
NOON
12:
1:00
1:
2:00
2:
3:00
3:
4:00
4:
5:00
5:
EVENING
6:00
6:
7:00
7:
8:00

SUNDAY DATE

AM
7:00
8:00
9:00
10:00
11:00
PM
NOON
1:00
2:00
3:00
4:00
5:00
6:00
7:00

This form lets you see your week's activities at a glance.

USING THE BOOK

Of course it is up to you to take the initial baby step and make the notations in the appropriate places in the book, which does everything *but* write down the information for you. If you use a book that you purchased do not get sidetracked trying to put every phone number in your life into the address section of the book. This transfer of information is not a priority. This is also why I have asked you to make your notebook. You can continue to use it (along with the Week-at-a-Glance calendar if you want) or, if you decide to purchase one of these books, you should be able simply to transfer the information from your notebook to the system of your choice. You will probably want to customize the system by making some changes so that the book fits your life-style and goals *exactly*. For example, I find that most of these planning systems put the goals and projects sections in the back of the book. I have moved them to the front of my book, just as you have written them at the beginning of your notebook. Because, before you plan your schedule, you schedule your plan, and this means planning your mission, goals, and projects. Writing them down and seeing them first, on a daily basis, helps to ensure that you don't forget the principle of making time in your life for truly meaningful activities and opportunities.

To plan your schedule for both the short term and the long term (weeks or months at a time) requires thought. For this reason, an appropriate system that you can carry with you can be helpful. Be certain to pick your planning system carefully. Don't buy a beautiful book that requires itty bitty handwriting unless you can write that way. Get a system that has, at the very least, goals and projects sections as well as at least monthly and weekly calendar sections. If you can't find what you want immediately, use your notebook. The important things are to write everything down, review your notes daily, and plan ahead as much as possible. After all, since you did write down your goals, it is only logical that you will also want to get into the habit of writing down your planned schedule: these plans will ultimately lead you to your goals.

And while these plans are leading to your goals (and in this case, your goal is to get organized), they will also help you *stay* organized and on track on a day-to-day basis, thus saving time and at the same time giving you more time in your life to do what is really important to you.

Once you have a planning system with the appropriate calendar for the month, week (and possibly day), you can begin to schedule the "to do" items from your project sheets.

But how do you figure out which, what, and who to put where on the calendar? How do you set priorities on a practical, day-to-day basis? And not only that, what do you do when all of your best-laid plans and intentions get blown out of the water by those constant, unexpected interruptions that invariably seem to gobble up the precious time in your life? And finally, how are you going to get the time to get organized on a daily basis with all of this other stuff going on?

The answer to those questions was already partially resolved when you decided to make the expenditure of your time correspond to your mission and your goals. At that particular juncture, in an effort to keep everything as simple as possible, you prioritized your goals; in this case, you gave your goal of "Getting Organized" a number-one priority. Not only that, you then turned that goal into a project and proceeded to systematically prioritize each "to do" item on your "Getting Organized" project. Now you need only go back to your "Getting Organized" project page, pick out the number-one priority "to do" on that page, look at your schedule, find a block of time big enough to accommodate that particular task, and write it down, thus scheduling it in your life.

Then, of course, you actually have to *do* it, which is something else again, and we'll get to that in Part II. Up to now we've been concerned primarily with where to find the *time* to do it in the first place. But by using this five-step plan, you now have the ability to change your life from one that is time-starved to one that is blessed with activities and opportunities. You should be able to reassess how you previously spent (or wasted) your time and come up with a way of life that is more sensible and tailored to you, thus eliminating life-robbing, time-wasting activities and interruptions.

Your routine daily activities as well as your advance weekly planned activities should be scheduled in, and around, your project "to dos." And as you place your "to do" items on your weekly or daily schedule, be sure to follow one very important rule: *be flexible.*

FLEXIBILITY

What this means is that you should not book every single minute of every day with obligations, responsibilities, and things to do. The fact is, your plan will never, never work if you overbook yourself. You must remember to leave spaces and gaps of time on the calendar with nothing written in. Then when something takes longer than anticipated, when you have a real crisis (as opposed to an interruption-inflicted crisis) and nobody but you can resolve it, you can juggle things around a bit, still accommodate everyone and everything, and live through the day to tell the tale. If you pencil in these pieces of "empty" time, and nothing comes along to eat that time up, consider yourself lucky and use that time for *yourself.* Go to a movie, take a nap, read, work on a pleasant project, whatever. Filling up unexpected gifts of time is never difficult—what kills you is fitting too much into too little time and then expecting things to turn out right.

Once you have laid out a sensible schedule for yourself, continue to plan your days around that schedule. And don't forget to write in time for yourself by specifically planning for things that you want to do. This might mean noting some of the following types of activities/opportunities:

Saturday	Tennis	10:00 A.M.
Sunday	Brunch with Susan	11:00 A.M.
Tuesday	Historical Society mixer	7:00 P.M.

Write these things down, and then honor them as if they were as important as all your other responsibilities, commitments, and miscellaneous life demands—because they are. For the time spent *on* yourself and *for* yourself is every bit as important as the time you give away to others, whether you give that time to your job or your family and friends. Studies show that people who spend all their time for the benefit of others or other concerns (such as work) at the very least tend to be cranky and overstressed and may develop health problems as well. So create some balance in your schedule by scheduling time, not just for responsibilities, but also for your own spiritual, physical, and emotional needs. Merely eliminating the constant barrage of daily confusion can, in itself, be a godsend. So the simple act of setting up a daily and weekly schedule is definitely a major step in finding the time to get organized and stay that way.

Once you have scheduled a "to do" from your project list and followed that up by actually (gasp!) getting it done, then you may mark off that "to do" item from the project page as well as from the daily schedule page. When all of the "to dos" from the "Getting Organized" project page are marked off, you can throw that page away because, hallelujah, you have successfully completed your project. This means that something of major importance in your life (getting organized) has been thought about, applied to the meaning in your life, planned, activated, and most important, done. Now you can go on to the other projects in your life that you would like to do, and, not only that, now you will be able to tackle these projects with clarity, determination, and the conviction that you are doing the right thing at exactly the right time.

REVIEW AND UPDATE

To assure a smooth planning process, once each day, preferably at the end of the day, take a few minutes to look at your schedule, mark off all the "to do" action items that you've completed, and then move the items that are not completed (for whatever reason) to another day on your schedule. At the same time, review your goals to make sure you are still on track and making wise use of your time on a daily basis.

Six

Procrastination

The beginning of the end

Let's see. You thought you were disorganized (or maybe the person who gave you this book thought so) but have now discovered you're not so bad after all. You've figured out your mission and your goals in life, and you've decided, on your own, to get your act together. Not only that, but you've scheduled a plan and planned a schedule. You're ready to get down to business and *get organized!* And you are going to do it, you really are, you say—

soon   *Later*

next week   **When I can fit it in**

AFTER I FINISH THESE OTHER PROJECTS

And, this book has been helpful, it really has, and you'll read the rest of it,

When I have the time

In the meantime, you'll just set the book, along with your organizational project plan, schedule, and good intentions, over on that pile you've got going of other reading materials that you have been meaning to get to. No, really, you are just going to put the book over there,

For now.

While you're doing that, why don't you just kiss the price of the book goodbye. In fact, you could have also saved yourself (or your friend) the trip to the bookstore (traffic was awful!) and the time it took you to read the first five chapters if you had just taken the money you spent and chucked it into the garbage disposal. Because, now that you are postponing what you have already started with this book, it has all been for naught.

And then, why don't you do this. Go down to the courthouse and get the necessary papers, and change your name from whatever it currently is to:

PETE or POLLY PROCRASTINATOR

Because I know, and deep down you know, that you are a hopeless procrastinator, and you can make all your lame excuses to other people you know, but I don't want to hear them. I know a procrastinator when I hear one. Personally, I think that procrastinators suffer from bad habits that all add up to postponeitis. I understand, however, that some say (some shrinks, that is) that procrastinators have an internal conflict of some sort or other going on. It doesn't take a medical genius to see that procrastinators aren't too big on success; I suppose you could say they *fear* success. Really, if you actually go ahead and *do* something, it just *might* be a roaring success, and then where would you be? You might have to actually live an exciting life, and gee, how do you do that?

Beats me. But I say, try it out, and if success and excitement come knocking on the door, you can figure out how to say hello when you open the door. If you are worried about failing, you are in good company. I don't know anybody, successful or not, who doesn't worry about failure. And nobody, but nobody, likes to fail. But if that's your worry, then train yourself to ask yourself this:

WHAT'S THE WORST THAT CAN HAPPEN?

Usually the answer to that question is not a big deal. Maybe you'll get a dose of rejection. A little rejection now and then is good for you—it builds character. Maybe you'll lose a little money. As long as it's not your last penny, take a chance. You could make a fortune, too. Maybe you won't get that promotion. So what? You're not going to get the promotion sitting on your duff, either. And anyway, there's no time like the present. You are not getting any younger, you know.

What's that, you say? I don't understand? Oh, but I do understand. If you don't procrastinate, anything can happen. And, if you do procrastinate, anything can happen as well. Let's talk about what can happen if you *do* procrastinate. I'll tell you a *true story* about my good friend, R. J.

THE STORY OF R.J.

R. J. was brilliant, and very, very creative. He was also a nice guy. His wife thought he was a nice guy, too, so she overlooked his constant tendency to procrastinate, until one bright and sunny day at 6:30 in the morning, when the marshals came banging on the door to collect her husband and take him away.

Good grief, how could this happen to R. J.? He's such a nice guy and certainly not a lawbreaker. The man doesn't even swear.

This is how it happened that the marshals came for R. J.

R. J. had entered into a little business deal with a client, June Anderson. R. J. was to provide June with a custom sofa, but due to one thing and another (a lot of it having to do with R. J.'s constant procrastination, but some of it having to do with June's lack of funds), June didn't get her sofa when she thought she should have. By the same token, R.J. didn't get his money when he thought he should have. June called R. J., but he almost never returned her calls (procrastination again). Finally June took R. J. to small-claims court.

Soon R. J. got an official-looking piece of paper in the mail saying that he should meet June in court on a date listed on the paper. R. J. and his wife looked at the date on the paper, looked at the calendar, and saw, or thought they saw, that the date was on a Sunday. Impossible, they said. "Well," said R. J. to his wife, "I'll just ignore this. June Anderson can't win anyway. After all, that blankety-blank woman owes me money!"

Three weeks later, the marshals came with a warrant for R. J., citing him with contempt of court. The marshals were nice enough, they really were, but R. J. couldn't understand why he couldn't shave and shower before they hauled him off. R. J.'s wife was mad as a snake that these marshals were in her house, and she was even madder at R. J. She *knew*, she was *certain*, that somehow R. J.'s procrastinating ways had brought these marshals to her door. And she was right.

R. J. was a really nice guy, remember, and when he got to court, (unshowered and unshaved), he told the judge he didn't understand, and the judge believed him. The judge dismissed the contempt charge and set another date for R. J. to come back and deal with June Anderson ("See to it that you show up this time!"), then let him go. But as R. J. walked out of the courthouse, the marshals grabbed him again, and this time they took him to *jail*.

R. J.'s procrastinating past had finally caught up with him, because the city computer had his proverbial number.

Four years before, R. J. had been driving his van merrily along when he was stopped for some infraction and subsequently ticketed for an expired driver's license. R. J. never took care of the ticket, and now, he *still* didn't have a driver's license. So now he was on his way downtown to one of Los Angeles's most notorious lockups, the county jail.

Finally, at 6:30 that night, he reached his wife. "Come get me, honey," he said plaintively. R. J.'s wife was a little bit of a sucker here, and she decided to drive downtown and bail R. J. out of jail. She'd give him a piece of her mind later.

So, downtown she went. She walked confidently up to the deputy and his computer. "I'm here to get R. J. out of jail," she said, with an embarrassed smile.

R. J.'s wife had her smile wiped right off her face when the deputy told her that the bail to spring R. J. was $1,000.

"How is that possible?" she asked sweetly. "R. J. is in jail due to a sofa mix-up and an ancient traffic ticket."

Not quite, the deputy informed her. Seems that since the contempt citation had been dismissed just that day, it was still on the computer at the county jail, even though the judge in Beverly Hills had told R. J. that he would overlook, or hold, the contempt citation so long as R. J. would promise to show up at the next court date. And, of course R. J. had promised. But the computer didn't care.

R. J. and his wife were not rich people. A thousand dollars was a lot of money and they did not have it. R. J.'s wife went home and called a friend of hers who was a lawyer.

"What should I do?" R. J.'s wife asked her friend the lawyer. The lawyer promised to call Beverly Hills in the morning to see if she could find out what was going on. Probably she could help with the computer mix-up, though it wouldn't be easy. With the procrastination issue, R. J. was on his own.

R. J.'s wife accepted that R. J. would spend the night in jail, and she went to bed. The cat slept on R. J.'s side of the bed that night.

At five the next morning, R. J. called collect from the county jail. "They told me you were here last night, and you left and didn't come back," he said weakly. R. J.'s wife told him not to worry, that their friend the lawyer was working on it, and she'd get R. J. out as soon as possible. R. J. had not slept all night, poor thing.

At 9:00 A.M., R. J.'s wife called the lawyer, who was already trying to straighten everything out in Beverly Hills. R. J.'s wife went to the bank, got some cash (not $1,000) and headed downtown to the county jail.

She went back in to see the deputy and his computer. Lo and behold, somehow the computer had corrected itself (probably thanks to the lawyer's efforts) and now the bail was a more realistic $136. R. J.'s wife paid the bail on the traffic ticket and waited at the door for R. J. Eventually the deputy yawned and informed R. J.'s wife that she was in for a long wait: to "process" a prisoner out the door could take anywhere from four to eight hours.

Finally, five hours later, R. J. walked out a free man. He went home, took a shower, and climbed gratefully into bed. R. J.'s wife decided that the time spent in jail had taught R. J. his lesson about procrastination and, mercifully, kept her mouth shut. She did not kill him, as she had previously planned.

Now that R. J. had spend an unpleasant but very enlightening thirty-four hours in the judicial system, watching the wheels of justice turn, ever so slowly, he thought maybe he should stop procrastinating and get the matters of the sofa and the 1981 traffic ticket cleared up.

So he went back to Beverly Hills on the appointed

court date, with the lawyer, to take care of the June Anderson sofa matter. June, because of R. J.'s initial procrastination and subsequent failure to appear at the court, had won a $1,500 judgment against R. J. Of course, now he owned the sofa, but he didn't need a sofa nearly as much as he needed the $1,500. And, let's not forget the lawyer, who, thank God, was a friend, but was costing money, too—$200, to be exact. Procrastinators *do* pay.

On the appointed day, R. J. went to another court, an hour's drive away, to take care of the 1981 traffic ticket. R. J.'s wife drove him, because R. J. *still* didn't have a driver's license.

When only fifteen people were left in the court-room, the judge gave a little speech. "Those of you who remain are people who did not pay your ticket, and then when you were summoned to court, you failed to appear. I could throw all of you back in jail if you don't have money for the fine, which can be any-where from $90 to $500." R. J.'s wife started to get ner-vous. "Then there's the matter of why you were stopped in the first place—you're going to get hit with a fine for that as well." Good grief, this was getting ex-pensive. "But I like to think," said the judge, "that most of you didn't *mean* to ignore your responsibilities, although it does cost the taxpayers money to round you up, and that irritates me no end." Now the *taxpay-ers* were involved in R. J.'s procrastinating ways. The judge concluded with "Let this be a lesson to you" and began calling the offenders forward.

R. J.'s wife noticed that the judge tended to let everyone go with a small fine, provided they announced "guilty" to the bench. Some quick arithmetic told her that it was likely that, based on the fines the judge was giving out, R. J. could walk out without paying any more than the bail money of $136, which the court already had in its possession.

Finally R. J. was called forward. The judge asked

for his driver's license. Of course R. J. didn't have one. "You have thirty days to get a license, or $25," said the judge. So far, so good. "Now, what about your failure to appear in 1981?" Whereupon, R. J. told the judge the story of the Beast.

"In 1981 I owned a dilapidated van that my wife and I dubbed 'the Beast.' The Beast broke down a lot, but I could fix it myself most of the time. Now the Beast was parked on the street and from time to time the streets get cleaned. Usually I would move the van to another parking spot when the street-cleaning day arrived, but sometimes the Beast was broken and I couldn't move it. So I got parking tickets. Then, one day the city came and towed the Beast away.

The city checked on its ownership and discovered $500 worth of parking tickets. I could either pay the tickets, or the Beast would be auctioned off. I decided I'd be way ahead if they sold. So all those parking tickets were wiped off my record when the city sold the Beast in late 1983."

"Why are you telling me this?" inquired an annoyed judge. "What has that got to do with driving without a license, and then your failure to appear in 1981?"

R. J. started to ramble on in what can only be described as procrastinator's poppycock. The judge stopped him again.

"Do you want to plead not guilty to this, is that what you are trying to tell me?" asked a now very tense judge.

"Yes, sir, not guilty," said R. J. ever so smartly.

R. J.'s wife stood up. She marched outside with him, fuming.

"Are you insane?" she screamed. "This whole thing could have been taken care of once and for all, *today*, and now you have to come all the way out here again next month and start all over again with this nonsense! And who knows how much it will cost you then? We both know you are guilty of procrastination on the driver's license *and* on the failure to appear." R. J.'s wife kept this up all the way home.

Next morning, he trotted on down to the Department of Motor Vehicles to get his driver's license replaced. He was stunned to find that he couldn't until he paid over $350 worth of parking tickets racked up on the Beast in 1984 and 1985.

"Whaddya mean?" asks an understandably perplexed R. J. "The city sold the Beast in 1983, and I don't even own it anymore, and I sure didn't own it in 1984 and 1985." Too bad, say the motor vehicle people, our computers don't show anything about a sale.

R. J. wrote letters and made phone calls—many of them long distance. Finally somebody in Sacramento told him to send $16.50, and they'd have their computer spit out the information R. J. needed. He sent the money, and Sacramento sent the information.

The new owner not only did not take care of doing the proper paperwork so that R. J.'s name would not be listed as owner, but left the Beast on the street to accumulate parking tickets until—you're not going to believe this—the city towed it away and threatened to sell it again in order to clear up the tickets that were outstanding. R. J. was furious at the new owner's procrastination.

It was one big mess, no doubt about that, and R. J. *still* didn't have his driver's license. And he certainly didn't have $350 to pay some other jerk's parking tickets.

R. J. did the only thing he could do. He called the court and sent a letter, asking them to let him plead guilty on the 1981 charge and apply the bail to his fine. The court said fine, kiss your $136 goodbye and try not to do this again.

Now all R. J. had to worry about was getting stopped for driving without a license, which he couldn't get because of the parking tickets on the Beast. And if he got stopped, he'd go to jail because of those parking tickets, and R. J. and his wife didn't have the money it would take to get him out of jail. Furthermore, R. J. had a strong suspicion that his wife would let him rot in jail this time, and that made R. J. very, very nervous.

And, oh yes, the Beast. Somehow the city needed to straighten out the fact that he didn't own the vehicle any more. Which he didn't. But since he never really went down in person (he kept putting it off) when they initially took the Beast in 1983, he really didn't have all the documentation that he needed. The city had it, though. Somewhere.

This is what the beginning of the end looks like. R. J. knew it, he felt it. As his wife would tell you that R. J.'s procrastination had cost him, in this matter alone,

- *$200 for a lawyer*

- *$136 for bail*

- *Thirty-four hours in jail*

- *$25 for phone calls to Sacramento*

- *$16.50 for paperwork in Sacramento*

- *Four hours in court in Beverly Hills*

- *Five hours to drive to court for the 1981 ticket (including the time it took R. J. to tell the van story and plead not guilty)*

- *Countless hours on the phone and at the typewriter to straighten out the mess with the Beast*

- *The van*

And that doesn't include the fact that R. J. is still liable for over $350 in parking tickets.

That's the story of R. J. He procrastinated on minor things—the traffic ticket, and not returning June Anderson's calls, and soon was squashed by a procrastinator's snowball of epic proportions.

So don't tell me you'll do it later, or soon, or when you can fit it in, or when you have the time (which you don't have now). Because I don't want to hear any more procrastinator's poppycock. If procrastination's got you paralyzed, try these tips to get you moving:

DO THE WORST FIRST

BREAK THINGS UP INTO BITE-SIZED PIECES

Tackle a project by working on it for an hour or two each day, instead of making yourself do it all at once.

CONSIDER YOUR ENERGY LEVEL

If you are a "morning" person, then you will want to do the worst, or the most difficult first, in the morning when you have the most energy. If you come alive in the evening, you'll want to save your difficult or dreaded tasks until then when you have the most energy.

REWARD YOURSELF

Reward yourself by working for a small period of time on a project, and *then* rewarding yourself, e.g., "I'm going to work on this for two hours, and then I'll watch television."

Those are a few tricks to help you off the path of procrastination. You really should put those tips to work, because the procrastinator's path in life is fraught with hazards that can definitely be the beginning of the end.

Just ask R. J.

Seven

Time Marches On

So, you've completed the five-step plan and grabbed onto some more time to get organized, and then you hit "the wall." Procrastination can sabotage the best of intentions each and every time, but you're a stronger person than that, and now you vow that you are not, repeat, *not,* going to procrastinate. Since you have carefully mapped out your plan to give yourself more time to pursue your goal of getting organized, you are now ready to get to it, except, hold the phone . . . uh, oh. You lived by your well-planned schedule for a week or so, and somehow, even though you thought you had a handle on the time problems, you now find that *you still don't have enough time to get organized*—and this in spite of the fact that we all know darned well that if you'd get yourself organized to begin with, you'd have even more time in your life.

Which reminds me of the time I was writing an article on how to save time at the bank and also avoid waiting in line. I interviewed a banker on the subject, and in the course of the conversation, he suggested that it would be helpful and time saving if customers came in with the necessary records when they applied for a loan or wanted to open a new account. When I asked Mr. Banker what records were required to open a bank account (in California), he told me that a California I.D. or driver's license plus a major bank card were necessary documentation in order to open an account. Stunned, I asked him how a customer could be expected to bring in a major bank card to open an account when, clearly, the customer didn't have an account in the first place and, in fact, the customer was there *to open an account.*

Mr. Banker had his answer ready. "Well yes, that is a problem." End of conversation. Mr. Banker, as well as his mighty bank, in my opinion, are part of the problem, not the solution.

I'm going to try to do a little better than that idiot, Mr. Banker. Between the insights about the need for getting organized, its costs, and the planning and/or procrastination involved, you really should have found some time that you didn't realize you had. Naturally you will use this time for getting organized. But we know that some of you need still more time in order to get the job done, probably in part because

TIME MARCHES ON

TIME FLIES WHEN YOU'RE HAVING FUN
(not to mention when you're getting older)

THERE'S NO TIME LIKE THE PRESENT

TIME WAITS FOR NO ONE

A STITCH IN TIME SAVES NINE

Time, when you get right down to it, is of the essence.

Huh? The essence of what? The essence of your *life*. Only you can stop the vicious, disorganized circle of never having enough time to get organized so that you never have enough time to do what needs to be done. One way to break the circle is to understand the rules.

TEN GOLDEN RULES OF TIME MANAGEMENT

1. UNDERSTAND THE VALUE OF YOUR TIME. Know that each moment of your life, once gone, is lost forever. Understand and develop the mission for your life, then live your life with that in mind, and plan to make each moment count.

2. MAKE PLANS. Set goals and deadlines that fit in with your mission, and then work toward fulfilling those goals. Lurching from day to day never produces much over the long haul. Remember, people don't plan failure, but they do plan success.

3. PRIORITIZE. Set priorities on a daily, as well as a long-term, basis. Remember that nearly every person and thing in your life has its own level of importance. Think about this, and set your priorities with that in mind.

4. LIST PROJECTS TO DO. Organize your time by putting your unfinished business (to do) list, an item at a time, on the proper project page and then the proper schedule page. Check off each item as it is done and revise the list periodically as needed. This routine provides you with a sense of accomplishment as well as organization, and it helps you plan and effectively prioritize, not only your schedule, but your life.

5. BUDGET YOUR TIME. Include time in your schedule for work, play, family, and spiritual matters, as well as regular time for yourself. A balanced life-style is more rewarding (and usually lasts longer) than an obsessive life-style.

6. BE FLEXIBLE. Unexpected things come up—disasters as well as delights. Leave some room for flexibility in your schedule, and you'll be able to handle the unexpected.

7. NO WAY! Learn to say *no*. Say it pleasantly, but firmly; never defensively. You cannot, nor should you have to, constantly accommodate everyone else's needs at the eventual expense of your own time and needs.

8. CHECK YOUR CALENDAR. Get a good appointment book or planning system that you feel comfortable with, and make it an integral part of your daily life. It is unrealistic to expect yourself to keep your entire schedule (the time of your life) accurately in your head. What are you, a human computer?

9. PERFECTLY IMPERFECT. Stop procrastinating, and compromise. Stop letting your sense of perfectionism keep you from doing something or letting someone else do it for you. Learn to compromise to get things done. Excellence is not the same as perfectionism! It has been proven that acute perfectionism almost invariably provides a barrier to success and personal satisfaction in one's life.

10. HELP! Hire others to do errands, secretarial work, housekeeping, bookkeeping, gardening, organizing, and anything else you can afford. At work, *delegate!* It is a fact that people who get lost in the details do not move up the ladder of career success. Let others do the things that you really don't have the time to do or don't really *want* to do.

Those Golden Rules should influence your life on every level. Carry them with you on a card, and when you feel yourself becoming overwhelmed, read the list again to remind yourself about, quite simply, the manner in which you are proceeding with the time that has been granted to you on this earth. This is your *life* we are talking about!

From now on, as the time in your life opens up and becomes more available to you (because you use time only for your purpose and goals, keep a time log, observe beeping watch reminders, or use any other method to change your poor time-management habits into good activities/opportunities management), you will *save* what you had previously *wasted*—time.

For an extra boost in the activities/opportunities (time-management) department, try incorporating the following time-saving tips into your schedule. They'll bring you even closer to your goal of getting and staying organized.

TIME TIPS

What Time Is It Anyway? Wear a reliable watch, and teach yourself to look at it regularly. When you buy a new car, get one with a clock. If you have an old car, buy a cheap digital clock that you can stick on the dash. Have at least one large, reliable clock in your home (other than the alarm clock) and a clock in your office. How can you manage your time if you never know what time it is?

Get Up Early. Get up earlier than usual, and give yourself plenty of time to get properly prepared for the day that awaits you. If you have a family, get up before they do so you can be ready for the human onslaught. That breakfast doesn't get on the table and those bodies out the door without your organizational help. Do yourself a favor and get organized *in advance*. If you've a career to tend to, getting up early will ensure that you are dressed properly and arrive on time. You might even go into the office early, before the phones start ringing and the interruptions start interrupting you every five minutes. You'll actually be able to get some work done and have an organized head start on your day.

Consolidate Tasks and Errands. Make a list of errands that can be done in the same shopping center or area of town so that you save time and gas with a one-trip consolidation. Tasks can also be grouped. If you get up to walk over to the pencil sharpener on someone else's desk, why are you taking only one pencil? Take several, and save yourself numerous time-wasting trips.

Where's the Scissors? Make your physical environment at work or home convenient for you by having frequently used items readily accessible, even if this means having more than one of the same item in different rooms and locations. Scissors, for example, are used in several different rooms from time to time—why spend time chasing after your only pair?

Freeze It. Make meals ahead of time and freeze them to use on heavy-schedule days. You can purchase compartmentalized containers, fill each compartment with the components that make up a complete meal (entree, vegetables, etc.), and freeze the meals in advance. You can even get some containers that go from freezer to microwave, and on a too-short day these instant, yet home-cooked meals can be real lifesavers—not to mention time-savers.

Send It Out. Send some of your laundry to the professional laundry. Count up how many hours you spend each week ironing and multiply that by fifty-two, then double that figure because it's so incredibly tedious. See what I mean? Go ahead, send it out. It's worth every penny.

Shop by Phone. Obtain all the major department-store catalogs, compare prices, and shop by phone. Besides saving time, you'll probably save money. You know when you go shopping you always see something else that you really didn't need but buy anyway. Like that amusing executive desk toy that so far has amused absolutely no one, and those outrageous black, on sale, fishnet pantyhose that you just *knew* would come in handy someday. Someday still hasn't arrived.

Check Labels. Stop buying cars, furniture, and other items that need special babying or care. It can be worth the time you spend to do a little research to find out which brand will require little special care. Low-maintenance living means more time for you.

Wish You Were Here. Use waiting time (such as at airport, subway, bus, or waiting for children) to read or write letters.

Is the Doctor In? He certainly is, but chances are he'll make you wait just about *forever* in his stuffy waiting room. To avoid this, insist on having the first appointment of the day. Instead of waiting two solid hours, you might get off with a mere thirty minutes. Doctors really do understand fully the value of time—their bills are clearly a reflection of that. I am waiting for the day that they wake up and realize that my time is valuable as well. Looks like a long wait.

Ready to Go. If you are frequently away overnight, keep a tote bag packed with essentials: toothbrush, soap, shampoo, razor, nightgown or pajamas, light robe, etc.

Start on Time. Start on time, even if others are late. Don't bother to rehash conversation that has already taken place before their arrival, and if it's dinner we're talking about, definitely do *not* reheat the food. You've got your own time-management problems; why should you accommodate others' mismanagement of their time?

What's the Agenda? Use a formal agenda for meetings, and then stick to the agenda religiously. People at meetings, as in life, have a tendency to get off the track, and when they do, you're pulled off the track as well. It's important to keep your sights fixed on the goals at hand and not let others' nonessential goals interfere with your intended purpose.

Bacon, and Over Easy, Please. Schedule breakfast

and lunch meetings instead of evening meetings. Breakfast meetings especially seem to wind up being more productive—the lack of available martinis might have a little something to do with it.

Thank You for Calling.   Buy an answering machine to screen your calls. The machine will handle your ex-husband (or wife), phone solicitors, and, heaven forbid, bill collectors with the utmost efficiency and dispatch. If you like, you can push the monitor button, hear who is calling, and pick up the phone to take calls you wish to receive. The rest of your precious time can be spent in a more productive manner, since you will be mercifully spared unnecessary and/or unpleasant interruptions.

Who's Calling?   If possible, return your phone calls all at the same time. Interruptions by the telephone tend to be nonproductive and distracting a good portion of the time. A phone machine or answering service can often be a lifesaver here.

Telephonitis.   Do your social chatting on the telephone while you are doing something else. Yakking on the phone is something that can actually perk up a dreadful session at the ironing board or the kitchen sink. Some other things you can do while you are talking (we're speaking about social talking here, not business calls) or on hold are:

FOLD THE LAUNDRY

FILE YOUR NAILS

CLEAN OUT YOUR WALLET

PULL OUTDATED CARDS OFF YOUR ROLODEX

BEGIN ORGANIZING A MISCELLANEOUS JUNK DRAWER NEAR THE PHONE

This Is a Recording.   Develop a few standard replies

to get off the telephone or end meetings. Some really top-notch standbys are:

I'D LOVE TO TALK, BUT I'M LATE FOR MY DOC-TOR'S APPOINTMENT.

I GOTTA GO, MY WIFE/HUSBAND IS WAITING AND HE/SHE IS GONNA KILL ME IF I DON'T GET OUT OF HERE.

I'M ON THE OTHER LINE.

I'M LATE FOR A MEETING.

I'M ON A DEADLINE.

And if none of these work on the telephone (my, what a persistent caller!), you can always hang up the phone in the middle of *your* sentence, thus making it appear that you got disconnected. Of course the caller will immediately ring back. Pick up the phone, and say "hello" three or four times before you say (all the while totally ignoring whatever the caller is saying on the other end), "Something's wrong with the phone again—there's no one on the line." Hang up the receiver and go back to work (or sleep). Of course, I've never been able to drum up the courage to actually do that, and I don't know anyone else who has been able to do it, either. I saw it done on television once and it was one of those things that looked like a good idea at the time, if you know what I mean.

Think Twice about Car Pooling. Car pooling is great for the environment, but if it means you have to stay at a particular function long after you would rather have left, perhaps you're better off driving yourself (or maybe not going at all). Even if all you want to do is leave early to catch up on sleep, it may be impossible to do so if you are at the mercy of another driver. This can also work with new dates. Think about this social advice:

Arrange to meet the person at the restaurant or theater. Then, if the evening starts to drag, you can leave before acute boredom or downright hatred sets in. "Dinner was lovely," you can say, ever so sweetly, "but I'm afraid I'm going to have to beg off on going to your friend's party [or, to your place for a nightcap]. I've got an early meeting at the office tomorrow that's very important." At that point you can either grab your own taxicab if you live in a big city, or drive your own car home, and get a blessed full night's sleep.

First Things First.   One thing at a time, if you please. Whenever possible, concentrate on one thing at a time to avoid fragmentation and disorganization.

Decisions, Decisions, Decisions.   Stop shuffling through papers, avoiding decisions. Don't avoid issues and problems. They merely compound, and sooner or later you have to deal with them anyway. They are always simpler to handle at the beginning. This applies to your dealings with people as well. Do you really think that the computer foul-up on your MasterCard bill is going to go away if you ignore it, or that you can take your time trying to get it corrected? Not only will it not go away, next month, if you wait, you'll be paying extra interest on the darned thing. And as for the people you have been avoiding, why do you keep stalling that nerd who keeps calling you for a date? You know you *never* want to go out with him, so why string the poor guy along? If you can't be honest, tell him you are married and be done with it.

Quiet Please!   Schedule time for yourself and your projects and call it your "quiet time." Train children and friends to respect this time, and thank them often for that. Be nice. Don't scream, "Shut up you brat, before I murder you!"

Get Rid of the Television Set.   Well, okay, I know this one is tough. It's probably un-American too. But you have to admit that if you got rid of the thing, you would definitely have more time. And if you have cable, and you get rid of the set, you'd save money, too. It's just an idea.

Great Idea!   Make an "Idea" section in your planning

notebook so you can write down those great ideas as they occur. You could be the next Einstein, but you'll never make it if you let those countless brilliant ideas get away from you.

Big Brother Is Here.   Invest in a computer. They really are faster and more efficient than the old ways of doing things. Of course you have to organize everything that is going onto the thing before you can transfer the stuff into the machine. That'll make you pause.

Refreshing Session.   Periodically stop and re-evaluate your goals and your schedule as well as how you have been spending your time. With the Ten Golden Rules of Time Management, use this evaluation session to reschedule, update, and reprioritize your time so that you can eliminate or cut down any backsliding you may have been doing.

Part 2

Organizing Your Space

Now that you've found the time to get organized, it's time to organize all the things around you. In addition to the clarity you've achieved by establishing your mission, goals, and projects, you found even more time through scheduling. Now you're going to follow your plan and "get physical" about getting organized.

As I've said before, if you have two weeks' vacation time available, the quickest way to get over the pain and anguish of it all is to go at it each and every day for fourteen days until it's *done*. If you don't have the vacation time and want to start right now, consider your weekend time. Be a bit more creative and see if you can't pull together some vacation time or sick leave or mental-health days (everybody needs a few of those!) and find a couple of long weekends comprised of three or four days at a stretch. Then give it your all during those days. Unplug the telephone, lay in some food, turn off the television, and get started. Remember that seven consecutive weekends add up to one fourteen-day vacation period and exact less than two months' time commitment from you— which means that you will complete your six-month goal, "Getting Organized," with four months to spare!

Your "Getting Organized" project page(s) in your planning notebook have already been broken down into such specifics as "Garage," "Closets," "Kitchen," "Office," "Paperwork," and so forth. If, for some mad impetuous reason, you haven't prioritized these segments of the projects, now would definitely be the time to do so. You should have gotten a reasonable head start on this in chapter 5, and by now you're probably yawning because, in fact, you've actually managed to cross off one or two "to dos." Gad, you're fabulous.

But of course, there's more to do, and the logical starting point seems to be your space—that is to say, your surroundings. As you know, sensible space planning makes it easier to organize getting organized. Naturally you'll want to be honest with yourself about your real trouble spots. You can always refer back to the quiz on pages 17-21 if you need to give yourself a gentle reminder. Take your vitamins, though, because no matter how you approach it, you'll want to do the worst first (oh yes you will).

Don't forget to stop now and again to revel in your success (so far) and maybe even give yourself a little reward from time to time. After all, who deserves it more than you do? In fact, yeah Rocko, put your fist in the air, turn on the music, and get ready to go. Victory looms just around the corner!

Eight

Making Your Space Work for You

It's probably an architectural plot. There's never enough space for ourselves and our things. Moving is one solution. That's the expensive solution, and it keeps the architects who plotted against us in the first place happy, happy, happy. Decorators too. Then there are the rent-gouging landlords, the banks who love big mortgages, and all the miscellaneous attendees to the problem: the maid, the repair people, the tax people, and on and on. But before you move, look around. There has to be *something* you can do about organizing the space you are already living or working with. With some of the following tips, maybe your place will be a candidate for a before-and-after photographic layout in *Architectural Digest* or *House Beautiful*.

But wait! Before you get started on the space problem,

take a long, hard look around the place. Do you still have a framed poster from college on the wall? Is your bathroom chartreuse? Do you have books from your hippie days that are no longer relevant, since you are now a successful stockbroker? And what about that lamp your mother gave you— you know, the one with the chipped base and the shade with the fringe on it? And check out your coffee table. Are you still stacking "coffee table" books on it? Don't you know that's passé? C'mon, we're gonna fix this place up to reflect your maturity, serene presence, and organizational sense. So, no, green plaid throw pillows do not work on the orange flowered sofa, and unless you plan to replace everything, you are better off ditching the pillows rather than the couch. You'll work around the orange flowers.

What about the bedroom? Does it always look like a war zone, with clothes, papers, books, and records piled everywhere? These things, strewn with such wild abandon all over the room, need to be organized and put away. Why buy sexy sheets when you can't even see the bed half the time?

So think about your space. This is your home (or office), and since you spend a substantial part of your life there, those surroundings should offer you a pleasant, peaceful, as well as functional sense of well-being. If you are into Zen, paint everything white and toss out the clutter. If you like collectibles, bring Grandma's things out of the garage—put those quilts on the bed and *use* them, and put some flowers into the antique vase you inherited from her. If you have just crossed over into your new hi-tech phase, go red, black, and gray. Get rid of the old to make way for the new.

While you are busy getting rid of the old, you might want to consider *not* replacing it with new. Probably the most basic understanding of how to organize effectively lies in knowing *what to throw away.* Don't choke. You can do it.

LEARN TO LET GO

One of the most difficult things to do as you organize is to learn to let go. As lives change, needs (wants?) change, but somehow objects accumulate with no regard to our changed perspective. Worn-out or out-of-style clothes, a pencil sharpener that hasn't worked for months, a five-year-old popcorn popper that you've never used because you hate popcorn, bundles of old letters and cards you'll never read twice, stacks of old *Glamour* magazines—these items should all be tossed out or given away. They are taking up valuable space and giving you nothing in return. Just because you like something doesn't necessarily mean you should keep it. Is it useful and functional? Do you want it or need it, and why? Does it serve a purpose or enhance your life in a meaningful way? If not, unless it has a very, very special meaning to you, *let it go.*

The most compelling reason I can think of to get rid of things is *less housework.* Don't you get sick of housework? Maybe you don't do housework. If you don't, count your lucky stars, because most of us do, and it uses up lots of precious time. One of the basic theories on the subject of clutter is that *the less you have, the less you have to clean.* Think about it. No knickknacks to clean. No books—you probably never look at them anyway—to dust, no glass coffee tables to spritz. Zowie! Freedom rings! That should inspire you to start tossing.

WANT VERSUS NEED

You might want to trash some things you "need" because you don't really *need* them, you just *want* them. Every time you pick something up and tell yourself you have to keep it because you *need* it, stop right there. Is this a need or a want? Mind you, there's really nothing wrong with *want*—that is, until it gets in the way of everything else. You'll have to make the distinction and the decision:

- *You* want *that old collection of 78 records that you haven't played in twenty years; you don't NEED them. (For Pete's sake, if you never play them, why do you want them?)*

- *You* want *those clothes in the closet that fit you three years and twenty pounds ago. You don't* need *them—after all, you can't even wear them! (Why* do *you want them—if you ever do lose that twenty pounds, the styles, or the cut and the fabric, will be wrong.)*

- *You* want *those old tax records from ten years ago. You must want them, because unless you are a very important crook, the IRS is not going to need them. (Why do you want these for heaven's sake?)*

Want versus need is a good thing to consider on all levels in one's life—for example, when other people are telling you that they *need* you, have to have you, for this or that reason. Do they really *need* you for the project, or do they just *want* you? If it's want they're talking about, then *why* do they want you? Is it because you are the only person who can do the job (unlikely), or is it because they are just plain lazy?

And how about that tricky trap known as shopping? Uh oh. This one gets me every time. Do you *want* or do you *need* that fabulous lizard datebook the clerk whipped out to show you when you stopped at the pen counter? It costs $200, and it's probably the skin of some endangered species, but, boy, oh boy, it sure looks nifty. You'd sure look organized and successful with this! Never mind that you have a perfectly good Week-at-a-Glance at home and at the office, which works like a dream for you. Forget that the lizard book is so small you'd have to scrunch up your fingers and write like a pigeon, you *want* that book. So you'll probably be a compulsive dope and charge it on some charge card that isn't quite up to the limit yet. But when you clean out your office, and come across that datebook that was never used, cost $200, is still not completely paid for, and consists of endangered lizard of some kind, remember that you *wanted* that book; you never *needed* it.

By asking yourself the want/need question, you can no doubt reduce the time you spend shopping by at least a third to a half (you'll save money, too, and that has to help your outlook). And you'll also save time because you won't have to spend so much time worrying about where to put, or how to organize, all of the stuff you have accumulated (and continue to accumulate). Because along with the worrying about getting organized goes the actual organizing itself—time consuming whether you do it daily or periodically.

So, determine if what you have is a need or a want, and if it's a want, ask yourself *why* you want it. If you're honest with yourself, your answers to the why question will be so stupid and embarrassing, that you'll get rid of a lot of things out of pure mortification.

Another reason to keep things is that you are *saving* them for some obscure reason. Again, ask yourself *why*. Really, are you taking them with you when you go? Are you saving them for someone else *after* you go? If you're saving them for someone else, that's a little cockeyed. Think about it. They may go before you do—it does happen, you know. Sounds morbid, but then saving a tablecloth locked away in a musty trunk until you die sounds morbid too. Put that cloth on the table, or give it to your loved ones for their table, or give it to someone who can't afford such finery. Let the tablecloth provide a loving backdrop for *someone's* meal. Don't store it if you don't use it!

Do It Yourself

Asking friends and relatives to help you with the project, by the way, is probably not the best idea. They won't be able to keep their comments and tacky little observations and philosophies to themselves, and who needs a steady monologue about what a disaster zone you are when, at that very moment, you are busy trying to, for God's sake, *get organized.*

So forget about calling in the troops for help. But do call them when the boxes of giveaways have all been assembled. They'll swoop down like a flock of vultures to take the stuff away. Mind you, this same stuff will be some of the things that they have been condemning you for keeping for lo, these many years. Resist the urge to point out their blatant hypocrisy as they are loading up their car with your castoffs. You will save the dump fee you would otherwise have had to pay, and the knowledge that you were right all along about the value of keeping the stuff will give you plenty of smug satisfaction for years to come.

THE GARAGE IS NOT THE ANSWER

Some of you may think you can avoid getting rid of things by packing them into cartons and stacking them in the garage. Let me assure you that you are only postponing the day of reckoning. Also, if you think "a place for everything, everything in its place," you'll realize that the *car,* not your high school yearbooks, belongs in the garage! (*Why* are you keeping those high school yearbooks?) On your mark, get ready, one, two, three, *toss!* And once you've tossed, remember why you did it in the first place

- LESS HOUSEWORK

- NEED VERSUS WANT

- SAVES TIME AND MONEY

- NO SENSE HOARDING—
  ENJOYMENT PASSED ON

Those are the same reasons that will keep you from reaccumulating another stash of meaningless miscellaneous belongings.

Now you are ready to organize your space. While you are organizing, do a little decorating. More than anything, your daily surroundings affect your outlook, and having an organized, pleasant home or office can make all the difference in how you approach each day. Remember that as you tackle the problem of organizing your space.

SYSTEMATICALLY ORGANIZE YOUR ENTIRE SPACE

Don't fool yourself into thinking that if you simply rearrange the desk, just so, over by an attractive window, and then clean out the drawers, you're organized. You must organize everything. When you start to clean out one area, you will need to have a place to put things, whether it's the filing cabinet or the kitchen cabinet. You'll definitely want to put things where they belong, but if, for example, your files are a disaster area, and you clean out the desk by shoving still more papers into the back of the filing cabinet, you are only moving your mess around and accomplishing nothing. The entire area—whether it's your home or your office—should be organized. Cleaning out a drawer here and there never works. Use the divide-and-conquer method and block out significant, relatively consecutive, segments of time to get each area completed.

Refer back to your notebook and your "Get Organized" project page. How was it prioritized? Was your office the first priority, or was it the kitchen? Tackle each area in the order that you prioritized it when you set up the project. Generally the "everything out first" rule will get you started. If you are doing your office area, pull miscellaneous things out of the drawers, and gather up all the papers on the credenza, bookcase, floor, and desk. Put everything in one large pile in a sorting area so that you can see how much space you really have to work with. Is there room in the bookcase for projects, or should that only be used for books? If the pile is enormous, that usually means you need to purchase additional storage—a filing cabinet or a storage cabinet for supplies, for example. But as you are emptying everything out, you'll find that much of it can be tossed, and there will be less left than you thought. With careful planning, and perhaps by moving a piece of furniture to make the room more functional, you probably can arrange things in a way that is automatically more organized. By taking the work a room at a time, and by moving things (papers, clothes, clutter) into one area so that you can actually *see* the room and its real possibilities, you should be able to stick to your space-organization plan. Not only that, you might just find that you like rearranging and organizing things, since the end result is often a much more pleasant room or area—one that not only garners positive comments from others but makes you feel better and more productive at the same time.

EVERYTHING IN ITS PLACE

As you work your way through each area on your project list, zealously tossing all that junk you don't really need, think about how you want your space to function, because the time-honored cliche "A place for everything, everything in its place" is going to be your organizational motto from now on. This means dirty clothes do not belong in the living room, file folders do not belong in a huge pile on the floor, and the blender does *not* belong in the bedroom! Think about the rooms things belong in and *keep* them there. If there's any question about where something belongs, put it in the area closest to where it's most likely to be used. And if you *never* use it, why are you worrying about where to put it? Get rid of it! Take a good hard look at how you're using your space and consider ways to make it serve your needs more effectively.

Use Available Systems. The outside world is just waiting for you to get organized. To help you, there are for sale, at a price of course, countless systems to help accommodate your things and solve your organizational problems. Check the appendices for more information. These systems can be installed in closets and cabinets and on the walls. If you rent, you can pull them out and take them with you when you move. If you own, these systems become an investment, since they enhance the value of your home.

Get It Up. Use wall space to store books, hang hooks for things that hang, and install shelves to hold everything from knickknacks to stationery. If you have a lot of nifty hats, put them in the hall, on hooks, in an artistic arrangement. Not only will they be nice to look at, they will remain in good condition, and you might even find yourself *wearing* them. Consider installing glass, Plexiglas, or wood shelves, either on a wall or in a corner to display your cat knickknack collection. (Don't forget, you'll have to spend time dusting those kitty cats.) Hang pots and pans on the wall. (No, they will *not* get greasy if you are using them all the time.) Be creative with the walls—they will gracefully accommodate much more than pictures.

Double-Duty Doors. Put a mirror on the bedroom door to dress by. Put hooks on the back of the bathroom door for robes, and hooks on the back of the bedroom door for other clothing. Hall-closet doors should have an extending rack on the inside so that you can hang more things inside the closet, and, depending on where your hall closet (or coat closet) is, you might put up an attractive hook on the outside of that door for hanging your coat when you first come into the house. Except for sliding doors, nearly all doors can give you double duty and provide you with more storage space.

Buy Functional Furniture. If you are buying furniture, try to make it functional. A nightstand, for example, should have a drawer and a shelf, or an enclosed storage space beneath it. Your television stand should have a solid shelf along the bottom for your clock, TV Guide, and whatever else you tend to keep near the TV. If you get a desk, make sure the drawers are ample for your needs. Functional furniture can be purchased in any style, from antique to hi-tech. You just have to look for it.

Organizing your space can be one of the most gratifying of all your organizing projects. You'll be amazed at what moving the furniture can do to make more effective use of the space. Just remember to schedule the project in your order of priority. Throw out or get rid of objects that you hate or that are just creating a space problem and aren't useful to you and your life-style. Then think about your space so that you can make it serve *your* needs. Asking the advice of friends and relatives often leads to some inspiring (free) ideas and can help motivate you to get started, since often their ideas are fresh (they've been afraid to mention them before), and you'll be anxious to complete the project so that you can revel in the results. Remember, your space is a reflection of you. With that in mind, work on your surroundings so that you can be completely comfortable with that reflection.

Nine

Homing in on the Housework

A word about housework. But just a word. Because believe me, housework is not, as they say, my area of expertise. In fact, I have found that lots of terribly disorganized people are fanatics about cleanliness, whereas I, though organized, can deal with a dirty bathroom better than most. That is to say, I can let it go for what is probably too long before I actually clean it.

But housework, of course, affects us all. Were we born in a barn? No siree, we were born somewhere near a house, and in a house (or apartment) we live. And whether we are organized or not, sooner or later the matter of the housework has to be dealt with.

For unless you are so privileged that someone else always does the housework for you, a substantial amount of your time, that is to say, your life, is probably *spent* on it. This may be an activity for our time, but c'mon, this can't possibly be an opportunity!

Let's say you spend the minimum amount of time on housework, which might work out to be 35 minutes each day. You may not spend those 35 minutes each day—but it's a fair guess that come Saturday, you'll add another concentrated six or seven hours on housework. In any case, your average 35 minutes per day, Monday through Friday, works out to 175 minutes, or nearly three hours per week on *housework*. Add seven hours on Saturday, and throw in another two hours for Sunday (cooking and ironing, and maybe a little mending), and you are now devoting a whopping twelve hours per week to housework, which may or may not be minimal in terms of time devoted to the dirty deed. By the end of the year, you will have spent 624 unrewarding hours, which comes to about twenty-six days total that you spent that particular year on housework—or nearly a *month* of your life each year! Check your yearly calendar. You're going to lose nearly a month of your life this year to that nonsense. Which month are you going to deduct?

And that twelve hours each week is really a very low estimate. This is based on the minimal stuff: wash the dishes on a daily basis, make the bed daily and change it once each week, do the laundry (you can kiss at least two hours goodbye right there), throw a little cleanser around in the bathroom now and then, sweep the kitchen floor when the debris starts causing minor falls and injuries, do the ironing, and when the spirit moves you, run the vacuum over the rug, the mop over the floor, and a dust rag over the furniture. Good grief, come to think of it, if you can do all that in *only* twelve hours each week, you get the Amazing Person award for housekeeping!

In any event, you'll want to organize the housework, because by doing this you'll gain more of that precious time you can use more delightfully in other areas of your life. Also, once you've organized your space, the maintenance of that space (housework) on a regular basis does contribute mightily to the overall organizational effort. There's no way around it, really—housework is a part of getting, being, and *staying* organized.

STAY ON TOP

Knowing that, here are some tips to keep the housework from becoming a full-time job.

Reduce Your Expectations.   Stop demanding that the place be perfectly clean and spotless. If it ever gets that way, it's a sure bet it won't stay that way, and why run like a rat on a treadmill if you don't have to? Try to train yourself to ignore the dust a little while. Cut back on your efforts here and there, and start adjusting yourself to a little less spit and polish so long as the basics are taken care of and the place is organized. Nobody will appreciate your housework efforts (much less understand them) but you. A little bit of a "who cares" attitude goes a long way in the housework department.

Schedule the Housework.   Make time to do the basics by putting housework on your schedule. Otherwise you might let it all go just a little too long and wake up one day to the Health Department banging shamelessly and very loudly on your front door. Work the housework in, and then get it done.

I'd like to be able to tell you that you can head up a project page in your notebook with "Housework" and then tell yourself that you'll get to that project when you're done with the other five projects you've already got going, but sorry, this is not a project. This (housework) is an ongoing, maintenance fact of life—like getting up and getting dressed. It really needs to be done regularly, which means that your schedule needs to accommodate it (unless of course you can afford to hire someone). The best thing to do, I think, is to spend thirty-five minutes (minimally) each day on housework, either in the morning or at the end of the day, to keep general maintenance under control (this does not include cooking). Then budget your weekend time (if you work) so that you schedule enough to do all the chores. If you resent the fact that you spend a substantial amount of your weekend time in this manner, try scheduling Thursday evenings for the laundry and Friday evenings for the marketing, giving yourself a little extra free time on Saturday, so that you don't have to get up to "go to work" on chores that day. Any way you do it will get results—so long as you're consistent in your scheduling to accommodate your housework needs. If you let things go, you'll be sorry—your mother-in-law or boss will show up unexpectedly when you are knee deep in dirty dishes and laundry. It never fails. Remember that housework is one of the areas of organization that takes very well to the divide-and-conquer approach—a little bit each day really does keep things under control.

Equality. Try to give each room that you clean an equal amount of time—say, twenty minutes per room. If you can't get the room cleaned in that amount of time, get a stopwatch, pretend you are training for the athletic event of your life, and work at it until you *can* do each room in twenty minutes. There is no room that deserves more than twenty minutes of your time (life) for housework. Maybe you can do one room in ten minutes. You clever devil. Now you've either got an extra ten minutes in your life for another activity or opportunity, or you can use that extra ten minutes in addition to the twenty-minute-per-room allocation on another room—for example, the kitchen.

Everybody Works. Yes indeedy, when it comes to housework, no one is too young, stupid, busy, or male to help out. Everybody in the house should pitch in, and they should also understand that their contribution is expected as part of their ongoing responsibility for themselves. You can buy several books on this subject alone, including *Confessions of a Happily Organized Family* by Deniece Schofield, and *The Sidetracked Home Executives* by Pam Young and Peggy Jones. And, if you can find it, one of the most brilliant books on the subject of housework, in my opinion, is *The I Hate to Housekeep Book,* written by Peg Bracken. This book was written, believe it or not, nearly twenty-five years ago and unfortunately is out of print. Along with a hefty sprinkling of household tips Bracken offers insight into the subject of housework that is hilarious and eternally appropriate—guaranteed to put housework in its proper place.

I'm Leaving Now.   If you're going out anyway, take the trash with you and dump it. Or take the dry cleaning. Or the mail. Whatever, just don't forget to group tasks and consolidate errands.

Buy Smart.   Every time you purchase anything, ask yourself, before you pay the cashier, how much time and money it is going to cost to have this item. Will you have to dust or clean it regularly? Does it have to go to the dry cleaner fifteen times each year? (Think about that one the next time you see a silk blouse "on sale.") Do you have a place to put it, or is it going to mean more clutter in your life? If it's furniture, make sure it does double duty. Otherwise don't buy it—you'll just end up cleaning it. Think, for Pete's sake. It'll save you time, housework, and money galore.

Get Rid of It.   This works well not only for housework but in terms of organization as well. If you get rid of something you don't really need, whether it's a porcelain cat figurine or a ten-year-old sweater you never wear, the fact is that you will never have to worry about cleaning or storing it again in this lifetime.

Get a Dishwasher.   I'm going to do this one myself. No sense continuing to operate in the Dark Ages.

Buy Paper Cups and Plates.   Stock up on these paper goods. You'd be amazed at the difference in dish duty (and, therefore *time saved*) even if all you do is drink your miscellaneous coffee, milk, water, soda, and other beverages out of paper cups instead of regular dishes.

Order In. I love these people. Pizza, chicken, deli platters. No muss, no fuss. And carry out works especially well when you want to give a party. Order a deli platter, get paper goods for the drinks and food to be served on, and pick out a fabulous dessert tray from some fancy-smancy place. Then hire the teenager next door to buzz around and pick up all this stuff (if they don't deliver). Give the party a name, like "A Picnic at the Jackson House," and relax and have fun at your own bash for a change.

Once Each Day. If you've got a family, do a load of wash each day. Throw it in when you get up. By the time you have showered and roused one and all from their beds, the load will be ready for the dryer. By the time everybody gets through breakfast, that load will be dry and ready to fold. Now make someone in the family (not you) fold the stuff. If kids on farms can milk cows before they go to school, then other kids on this earth can fold a few clothes before they tear out of the house.

Hire Someone Else to Do It. In my opinion this is by far the best of all ways to do the housework. Beg, borrow, steal the money to pay another person to do this work for you. Remember that you are paying for more than an additional month of time for yourself each and every year. At the end of ten years, you have roughly ten months' time you might have otherwise lost to housework. Whoopee. Fly to Rio and take an extended vacation. Be sure to stay someplace where someone else does the housework for you.

Warning: Don't expect a housekeeper or cleaning person to be able to get a handle on your *organizational* problem. Wise up. They were put on this earth, and sent to you, to *housekeep* and to *clean* as their profession, not to organize. (They probably think you're not operating with both oars in the water.) Ultimately, you are responsible for getting your *own* act together. Consider the true story of Mary Thompson.

Mary was one of the arty tribe. Apartment cluttered, with purple balls hanging from the ceiling—an apartment that was, in one sense, ordered but, at the same time, not. It was filled with things precariously balanced on window sills and on top of bottles. Miss Thompson's cleaning woman suffered this for eight months, but finally she quit. When asked why by a rather dismayed Mary Thompson, the lady came up with a precious, yet unanswerable reason for quitting: "God told me not to work for you anymore!"

Pick Up. If you can't do anything else, give the place a quick pickup. Getting rid of the clutter will make you think it is cleaner than it really is, and there are always a few minutes here and there to straighten the living room or the bedroom. Remember, doing something is better than doing nothing at all.

How Soon Will It Get Dirty? Don't clean something if it isn't dirty. It will be dirty soon enough, believe me.

That's about it in the housework minor-miracle department. I'm a firm believer, as I said, in reducing your expectations where housework is concerned—I've done it and, with a little practice, so can you. Once you've done that, it will be relatively easy for you to do the job quickly and quit as soon as it looks like you're even a little bit ahead. Until they start passing out awards for excellence in housework, my advice is not to worry about it too much, because, let's face it, the housework is not the least bit worried about you. While you do need to keep at the work regularly (albeit minimally), you don't have to devote a substantial portion of your life each year to it. Live a little. It's later than you think.

Ten

Clearing Up the Kitchen Clutter

Creative cooking is an art, but it's tough to be artistic when your "studio" looks like a disaster zone. It's even more difficult to come up with a meal that represents an act of love when you know for an absolute fact that your kitchen hates you. Kitchens are, more often than not, inadequately designed to begin with. Add to that the daily clutter that includes appliances, dishes, pots and pans, recipes, coupons, utensils, and much, much more, and you've got a good case of the kitchen clutters.

I won't even go into the meaning of cooking. Some of us can cook, and some of us can't. Some of us would like to cook—we think—but we don't really know where to begin. (Clearing off the counter might be a start.) I've always been told, rather scornfully, that if you can read, you can cook. I'm living proof that that statement is hopelessly incorrect. I can read, and I still can't cook. I took a Polaroid of the last little item that I tried to whip up because a relative told me it was so simple that "any idiot could cook it." That photograph is tacked to my kitchen wall, over the stove, where it reigns supreme—conceptual, pop, New Wave, final, artistic testament to my failure as a cook.

And yet, even though I don't cook, or maybe especially because of that, I find that an organized kitchen makes life happily efficient. After all, whipping up a fried egg sandwich (one of my specialties) is a ninety-second experience in an organized kitchen, whereas in a disorganized kitchen that same gourmet delight will take five minutes to prepare.

As for those incredible people who are wonderful cooks, the mind boggles at their many complex kitchen needs and aids. I mean, they stir up this and season that, virtually simultaneously. And somehow that cute little sprig of whatever gets cut and placed artfully on the plate, and the fresh linen napkins come out. And the food, ah well, the food is an experience in itself. For, even though I don't cook, I do love fine food, and I turn green with envy at the talents of the truly fine cook.

And what about the person who cooks for a family? Here's someone who turns out food for the entire bunch, night after night, invariably serving up a meal that's tasty, nutritious, and organized. This cook gets everyone to the table at one time (well, usually) and then manages to have somehow perfectly orchestrated the cooking process so that the food can be served all at the same time. Organizational and creative magic, if you ask me.

But whether you are a gourmet chef, a fast-food cook for the troops, or a noncook who prepares food only to survive, having an organized kitchen can reduce the aggravation that clutter and confusion invariably dish up to even the most stoic eater. Cleanup, always a hated process, becomes a bit easier when the kitchen is basically organized to start with. Everybody has a kitchen to prepare food in, and everybody, sooner or later, has to eat.

An organized kitchen will give you more time. It will enhance your creative cooking (in)abilities and make cleaning and maintaining order in the eating room much easier. (Especially if you are one of those who opens the refrigerator and eats something right there, standing—what is this, a bus stop?)

Check back to your "Get Organized" project page and refer to your "Organize the Kitchen" segment of the project. Do you want to clean it all out, or have you broken it down into steps that might include the more time-consuming projects, like "Organize My Recipes" or "Sort Through All of the Coupons"? If you have those types of mini-project outlines, you will have to decide which project you want to tackle first—the cupboards or the recipe organization. (Could your teenager organize the recipes for you, or could you do it a bit at a time in the evenings while you watch TV?) You will start in the kitchen based on your decision of priority.

TIPS FOR AN ORGANIZED KITCHEN

Whatever your kitchen looks like, and whatever your diet, these tips should help you organize the kitchen so you can feed yourself (and those around you) with a minimum expenditure of time and fuss:

Togetherness. Keep items as close to their functional area as possible. Keep pots and pans, pot holders, spices, and large cooking utensils near the stove. Knives should be near the cutting board, cups by the coffee pot, dish towels near the sink, and so forth. These arrangements save many steps and make cooking as well as cleaning the kitchen much easier on a daily basis.

It Used to Work Great. If it doesn't work, either get it fixed or get rid of it. A blender that is on the fritz does you no good. It only takes up space and wastes your time, because now that it's broken you have to do things by hand.

Hang It All.   Use any available wall space. Hang your pots, pans, large utensils, pot holders, lobster molds, and the like on the wall. You can install a pegboard (painted to match the decor) or buy hooks to make use of small or odd-sized available wall space. And for all of you fanatical Mr. & Mrs. Cleans out there, no, you will not have greasy pans, because you will use them almost daily, which means they will be getting washed daily, which means, as I said in the first place, the pans will *not* get greasy!

Merry-Go-Round.   Use lazy Susan systems in the cupboards. These washable plastic gadgets can hold everything from cleaning supplies to vitamins. They eliminate rummaging in the cabinets to find what you need (which is always, it seems, behind everything else).

Add Space.   Add another shelf under the sink. There's usually enough wasted space to do this, and while you've got your head under there, install a rack to hold cans (such as the cleanser) on the inside of the cabinet door.

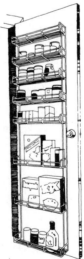

Racks like this one by Closet Maid can reduce kitchen clutter.

Closet Maid Storage Systems by Clairson International, Ocala, Florida

Clear the Decks.   Only store things that you virtually *never* use in hard-to-reach places (kitchens are loaded with inaccessible places—makes you wonder about the intelligence of the average architect). Things stored in the upper reaches of the cabinet are out of sight and therefore out of mind. Remember that the next time you crawl, like some deranged acrobat, up onto the counter to get something that you never should have put up there in the first place.

Step Up. Keep a collapsible step stool in the kitchen. You'll be amazed at the many opportunities you will have to use it. It will also save you from possible serious injury when you fall, with an ominous thud, off the counter top, where you crawled because you were too lazy to go round up a chair.

Away from It All. Good china, crystal, and silver that are only used on very special occasions should be stored in cabinets farthest from the actual work area in the kitchen, or in the buffet if you have one (after all, that's what buffets are *for*). But while you are storing this stuff you might want to make sure that you really *enjoy* acting as a holding and storage facility for things that you almost never use. Just a thought. I'm not saying you should toss the silver and crystal. I'm just saying you might want to think about what you get out of it only two times each year (Thanksgiving and Christmas) that makes it worth all the fuss.

Paper Drive. Don't store newspapers and paper bags between the refrigerator and the wall. They attract bugs and dirt, and eventually the bags and papers will expand into an unsightly mess. When have you ever used more than one paper bag or old newspaper in a month's time? Throw them out!

Trash with Dash. Use a large straw basket with a lid for a trash can; line it with a heavy-duty trash bag that you can lift out when it gets full. In the meantime, you are spared the daily vision of the trash as it accumulates, and you don't have to stash the trash can under the sink, wasting valuable cabinet space.

Shelving a Problem. Put your cookbooks on a shelf rather than on the counter, and unless you are going to put your clipped recipes (from newspapers, magazines, and grandmas and mothers-in-law), *in order*, and then follow that up by actually *using* those recipes on a fairly regular basis, *don't clip the buggers in the first place.* Because if you do, that one bulging drawer of yellowing, never used recipes will multiply to fill two or three drawers that you could be using to store something else that you *use.*

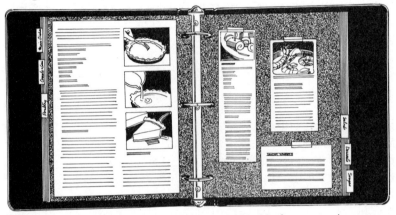

Your family recipes never looked better. This binder system is guaranteed to keep all of your recipes in order and instantly accessible.

Recipe Library. Here's a solution for your clipped recipes: Buy one of those large three-ring binders that salespeople use for display and presentation purposes. This type of binder is covered in a plastic that allows the salesperson to slip a piece of presentation paper onto the front of the binder. It's going to allow *you* to keep the thing clean. Next, buy a box of clear plastic sheet protectors. Both the binders and sheet protectors are available at your office supply store. Organize your recipes by category, such as cookies, entrées, cakes, vegetables. Then slip each recipe into a sheet protector and staple it to the black piece of paper inside the plastic. If your recipes are written on two sides of the paper or card, simply remove the black insert sheet from inside the plastic sheet protector and staple the recipe to the plastic. This way, all you have to do is flip the sheet protector over to see the rest of the printed (or written) recipe. Separate the categories by putting index dividers between them. Now you have a cookbook that can be expanded at any time (or weeded out) and can be wiped clean. It's simple to add recipes to the proper category, and if you wish, you can snap one of the sheet protectors out of the binder and work from that one easy-to-clean page, thus eliminating the need to have the bulky book on the counter while you are working. If your collection is extensive, you might want to have separate binders for different categories. Any way you look at it, this book accommodates all recipes, whether they're on scraps of paper or they take up an entire magazine page. Just clip and staple. No more recopying onto those stupid little index cards that will forever be misplaced.

Could I See the Menu, Please? Sit down once a week and plan your menu for the entire week. Your week will go much more smoothly and pleasantly once that is decided and taken care of.

To Market We Go. Plan only one visit to the market each week. Then try to go during the weird times. I love Saturday night at around 9:30-10:00 P.M. Nobody's there but a few nuts, and I breeze right through the checkout counter. Find out what the off-peak hours are at your market, and save time by shopping at those times.

Stick to Your List. Stick to your well-planned list of things you need at the market. Getting sidetracked by supermarket displays will only distract you, and you'll find yourself running back to the market later in the week for something that was on the list but was relatively boring, like toilet paper.

And don't go to the market when you're hungry! You'll waste money *and* time; although you'll come back with the smoked oysters that you can eat *right now*, you will have forgotten the coffee you need in the morning.

Running Out. When was the last time you were in the middle of cooking something and reached for an ingredient, only to find you were out of that particular item? Rats! You can avoid such difficulties by keeping a pad and pencil on the kitchen counter and jotting down items you need when you see you are *running out* of that item. Don't wait until you are *totally out* to make a note of it. By that time, it's too late, and you're off to the store on yet another emergency trip for one item. To save time and avoid those needless trips, write it down *before* you run out of something altogether—and, guess what, you'll never run out of things.

I'd Like That Delivered, Please. Have milk, bread, and liquor delivered. If the store doesn't offer delivery, find a service, even if it's only the kid next door who'll be your own personal delivery service (except for the liquor).

What a Crock. Throw some stuff (as in food) into the Crock-Pot in the morning before you set off on your day. Your dinner will be waiting for you when you come home. It's heavenly to walk in to the smell of dinner cooking—and *you* cooked it!

Leftover Lesson. Store leftovers in the refrigerator in plastic Tupperware containers. These save room, can often be stacked, and if the contents are visible, there's a good chance that the food will be eaten. Food lurking in covered dishes or wrapped in foil inevitably gets pushed to the back of the refrigerator—only to be disgustingly discovered when you finally decide to clean out the fridge. (More information on containers and gadgets for the kitchen is in Appendix B.) Or *cook double*. Cook enough to serve and enough to freeze. You've saved yourself the time it takes to cook one whole meal. Zowie! You might want to cook some things up at the start of the week (maybe Sunday) such as casseroles, spaghetti sauce, meat loaf, that type of thing. Then, throughout the week, there will be plenty to prepare with only a few minutes' effort on your part. For instance, you'll only need to cook the noodles for the spaghetti, make some gravy and heat up the meat loaf, and so forth.

Freeze It. Make meals ahead of time and freeze them to use on heavy-schedule days. You can use compartmentalized trays (check places like Tupperware for these) to freeze meals you have made yourself. For instance, make up several vegetables, a meat loaf, and a chicken. Then divide the portions into the trays and bingo, you've got lots of well-balanced meals ready to pop into the oven and eat, and with only one cooking session in the kitchen.

Measure the Time You Save. Have more than one set of measuring spoons and keep them where you use them, such as in the coffee canister, the sugar tin, and the flour bin. The extra few dollars you spend will save you lots of extra steps in the kitchen.

Speedy Spicy. Organize your spices alphabetically. You'll be able to grab the spice you need without your customary groping.

Messy, Messy. Cook in an extra-large container so that it doesn't slop or boil over, thus requiring extra time to clean up the stove or oven.

Put Things Away After Using Them, and Clean as You Go. I can't cook, but I never forgot this one. My father once asked me what was the most important thing to know about cooking. I smartly responded, "To clean up your mess as you go along." I promptly got a dollar, and I never forgot it. You can clean as you go, while things are simmering and so forth, and your reward will be less time in the kitchen after the meal, when nobody I know wants to be in the kitchen—we all want to be flopped on the couch relaxing.

Say, Busboy! Use a dishpan or litter pan to bus dishes from the dining room to the kitchen rather than carrying one or two items at a time. This saves time and steps. Another good idea is to make other members of the family bus the dishes with the nifty litter pan or dishpan. Remember, delegate. It's the best time-saver of all.

Date Freeze. Wrap and date items that go into the freezer. Put each new item in the *back* of the freezer, thus moving everything else forward. The food will automatically present itself in order to you, and the chances of overlooking something until it spoils are significantly reduced.

Match It Up. If you are the type who keeps empty plastic containers such as margarine tubs (I know, I know, you can *use* those), then I'll bet you spend lots of time fumbling around trying to figure which lid goes to which bottom. An easy time-saving solution is to mark the tops and bottoms of the containers with a permanent marker so that you can easily match up the #1 lid with the #1 bottom. Of course, one could go a bit whacko on this one. What if your inventory is so great that you can't remember how many containers you have, which means that when you add another (totally unneeded) container to the stash, you won't know what number to give it (after all you don't want to duplicate numbers—that would only confuse your little self). Do yourself a favor and keep the plastic container inventory down to a reasonable limit. Otherwise you'll need a computer for the inventory and the mathematics.

You'll Wonder Where the Yellow Went. If you don't already have it, get a no-wax floor installed. You can get the tiles and do it yourself (I did), and it will vastly improve your life. Life is too short to spend a substantial portion of it waxing, or perversely, diligently removing the yellow residue of the old wax build-up that seems to imbed itself stubbornly into kitchen floors.

Automate. I'll say it again: get an automatic dishwasher! There is nothing so wonderfully organized as having someone or something else doing the dishes. What are you waiting for?

Zap Yer Food. Get a microwave. It zaps your food and cooks it in a wink of your exhausted eye. I'm a little nervous about zapped food, but it sure saves a lot of time at the end of an exhausting day.

Finally, You Can Hire or Marry Someone Who Does All the Cooking and Won't Let You Near the Kitchen. That's what I did.

Eleven

Out of the Closet

This chapter is for those of you who invariably jump up out of bed, late as usual, and dive into the closet, hoping to come up with something appropriate for an important appointment that day. *If* you can grab it instantly, I'd like to know what kind of condition it's in. I'd be willing to bet that those of you with disorganized closets do a lot of last-minute ironing. None of this ironing once a week for you. You've got a system whereby some things never get ironed until five minutes before they're to be worn, and things that come back from the cleaners, supposedly freshly pressed, always need a touch-up before you jump into them because you crammed the garments into the closet when you brought them into the house.

There's also the certainty that if you keep something long enough it will come back into style, that all you need to do is lose fifteen pounds and you will be able to fit into at least a third of all the things hanging there that you can't currently wear, and that if you could find the perfect blouse, it would go with those three skirts that you never wear because you don't have a blouse to go with any of them. What makes all of this so confounding is that you have a closet full of clothes and absolutely nothing to wear!

What about the hall closet or the spare closet? They contain tennis rackets, hiking boots, shopping bags of something or other, the cat kennel, suitcases, a box or two of important papers, two broken umbrellas and one umbrella that actually works, a throw rug you really don't care for (which is why it isn't on the floor where it belongs), lots of spare hangers all tangled up in one gigantic wire mess, and your coats and hats and a scarf or two. And, oh yes, the vacuum cleaner, which, every time you pull it out starts this incredible cascading effect that wreaks havoc you really don't have time for, and so, of course, you don't vacuum unless the cat has thrown up a bigger hair ball than usual and company is coming.

KILLER CLOSETS

These attitudes and habits all add up to killer closets. How on earth are you going to dress for success when you have a self-destructive conspiracy forming all by itself inside your closets? The fact is, no house or apartment really has enough closet space for most of us, so how you organize your closets and what you put in them can make a significant difference in your image, not to mention your life.

Then there's the one about first impressions (frankly, I can't remember the one about first impressions), but any fool knows that if you go to work in an outfit that doesn't match, or is wrinkled, or just plain looks stupid, you are definitely going to make an impression, and probably not the impression you had in mind. Plus, when you look stupid and outdated or un-put-together, you *feel* stupid, outdated, and un-put-together. And who needs that? After all, we can turn to our parents, our sisters and brothers, our children, lovers or spouses, and even our employers (good-bye fast track!) to get that feeling about ourselves. Sooner or later somebody is sure to clue you in on the fact that you don't have an ounce of class, and if they're really on a roll, they'll continue by telling you on what level specifically your total lack of class manifests itself. Whaddya wanna let your closet do the same thing to you for?

And for those of you whose schedule is so packed that you barely have the strength (not to mention the time) in the morning to run the iron over that hastily grabbed shirt or blouse, you'd better check your watch again. It takes five minutes at least to iron a shirt or blouse. Add to that another three minutes to set up the board, find the iron, the spray starch, and the extension cord; and fill the iron with water. Give yourself another two minutes to locate a clean shirt or blouse to actually iron, and now you have already wasted a full *ten minutes!* Multiply that times five days, and you have just given yourself fifty minutes that you didn't know you had. Yeah, you pout, but who is going to iron the shirts and the blouses? You don't have enough time as it is. Send them to the cleaners this week, and instead of sleeping until 11:00 A.M. on Sunday morning, get up at 8:00, and allow those three hours to clean out your closet.

And, consider this:

You can take the kids to your mother's for the day and send your spouse out to the golf course or the shopping mall. That ensures that you won't be bothered with a million interruptions. Or you can cancel that golf game (if that's what you originally had planned—and canceling it this one time won't kill you) and apply yourself to those dress-for-success shirts, pants, ties, belts, and shoes that make up the mess in your closet. In fact, one of the reasons you are probably so big on golf is that the only clothes you can readily lay your hands on in the closet right now are the golf clothes—mainly because they are lime green and lemon yellow in color and jump out at you no matter what condition the rest of the closet is in.

While you are rounding up snippets of time, you really should be annoyed at yourself. Because if you had followed

Before

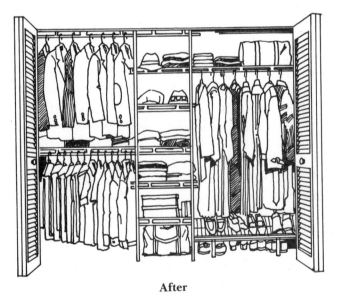

After

Courtesy of The Closet Store, Los Angeles, California

Disorganized closets can be transformed with the installation of a simple space-saving closet system.

the plan that we made in the first half of this book, you would have made the time for your "Getting Organized" then. You would have blocked it out in consecutive parcels of time that included full weekends committed to the task at hand (getting organized). So go back to your original weekend or vacation get-organized plan and add these extra bits of time to the hours you have already given away this Sunday (for the golf game and sleeping late), and take all that time together and write it down on your schedule, right now, while you're thinking about it. Next Sunday, here is what you do.

CLOSET COUNTDOWN

First and foremost, tell yourself this: "I am going to clean out my closet and get rid of all the clothing that is inappropriate for my current life-style. Since that pile of inappropriateness might be rather substantial, I am then going to reward myself by taking myself out to the department store where I am going to shop myself stupid." And if your budget won't accommodate this shopping spree right away, you can tell yourself that you are going to save yourself gobs of time (you won't have to wade through all those clothes, most of which don't look too terribly good on you), and you'll always look fabulous, because, even if you only leave yourself six or eight fabulous outfits for work and five or six for play, those few outfits are all going to make you look and feel so terrific that you can *wait* to go shopping.

See how easy it is to get motivated? All right, here we go:

Take Everything Out of the Closet. That's right, everything. You'll be amazed at the discoveries you'll make. Things that you thought were lost forever will turn up—you'll swear it's a miracle.

All or Nothing. Determine to do the job in one session. The notion that you can do a little bit here and there in the closet never works. What do you think will happen if you spend one Sunday cleaning off the first shelf on the right-hand side and vow to do the second shelf on the right-hand side the following Saturday? Pay attention, this is a quiz. By the time the second Saturday has rolled around, what has happened to the first shelf on the right-hand side that you cleaned the Sunday before? (And by the way, if all you did last Sunday was one shelf, what for Pete's sake did you do with the rest of your day?) That's right, you have shoved more junk onto that shelf, and now you are back to square one, the beginning. And where on earth did you put the stuff that you took from that right-hand shelf last Sunday?

You've Got to Have Friends. Have a friend help you. Now I know that I have put down your friends in the earlier parts of this book—you know, the ones I told you about who are always the first to point out your poor taste in clothes and who sneer and tell you in one way or another what a slob you are. In the case of closets, these are definitely the people to call. These friends, you see, will happily sit with you on a Sunday and laugh hysterically at your letter sweater from the class of '64, and the miniskirt from '72, that you are still convinced will be in style some day real soon. They'll also shake their head with an ominous "no way" when you hold up all those darling little outfits that fit you perfectly three years and twenty pounds ago. You may think that having that person there to help you is cruel, but believe me, it's for *your own good.*

Two Years, Tops. If you haven't worn it in two years, get rid of the silly thing. What are you, a thrift shop? I'll never forget the time I gave a speech at a successful buying office at the California Mart. The audience was made up of people who were in the fashion business. Sure enough, one woman piped up and said, "Well, but some things I keep because they are classic." If it's such a classic, why aren't you wearing it? This very same woman claimed that if she held on to anything long enough it would come back into style. That's patently ridiculous. In the first place, although styles do recycle themselves, the fabric and cut are always slightly different. And if your weight is the same now as it was seven years ago, then I'd like to know your magic secret.

Get Rid of the Garment If It Is:

TOO SMALL

TOO DATED

TOO FADED

TORN AND NOT FIXABLE

NOT WEARABLE BECAUSE IT DOESN'T GO WITH ANYTHING

JUST NOT YOU

You have several options when it comes to "getting rid of" your clothes. There's always charity, of course, from the Salvation Army to a shelter for the homeless. Then there's ye olde garage sale, which, if it won't hurt your feelings to see that skirt you paid so much for go for $3.50, is not a bad idea. But if you decide on the garage-sale method, make sure that you price everything at next-to-nothing prices, and at the end of the day, the leftovers go into your car and get transported directly to your local charity. Do not take the clothes back inside the house and hang them back in the closet! Otherwise you'll end up like the woman who told me that it was her *husband's* closet that was impossible, not hers. Finally one day, after substantial nagging on her part, her husband announced that he was going to clean out and organize his closet. Which he did. At the end of the project, he went downstairs, and proudly invited his wife to come up into the bedroom so that he could show her what he had done. "I put all the clothes I *usually* wear in this closet right here," he said beaming, "and I put all the clothes I *never* wear in this closet over here!" I rest my case.

Fix It. If something needs repairing, then get it repaired. Don't put it back in the closet until you (have someone else) repair it. Put it by the door, and when you go out, take it with you and drop it off at the tailor or shoemaker or dry cleaner.

Less Is More. Try to organize a wardrobe that goes with itself. Lots of skirts that are so weird they don't go with any blouses you have, and shoes in colors like fuchsia or mint green don't make much sense unless you are heavily into New Wave, or Old New Wave, or fifties psychedelic fashion. Try to have a few interchangeable, well-fitting, comfortable clothes that you are always happy to put on instead of a closet full of fads.

ORGANIZING WHAT'S LEFT

Categorize. Hang clothes in categories:

PANTS

SKIRTS

TOPS

DRESSES

JACKETS

SUITS

ATHLETIC CLOTHES

DRESSY CLOTHES

LINGERIE

SWEATERS (if you hang them)

SHOES

ACCESSORIES

Color Palette.   Hang the categories grouped by color. This makes selecting and coordinating outfits much quicker and easier.

Happy Feet.   Put all your shoes on a shoe rack—either one that hangs over the inside of the closet door or one that sits on the closet floor. The metal racks are far and away the best shoe holders. They are sturdy and give you a look at your choices for footwear at a glance. While you're at it, you might as well decide to grow up and get rid of all the shoes that pinch your feet and throw your back out. Toss those cute cowboy boots that give you blisters every time you wear them, too. Are you sick, or just plain crazy? Don't you know that you really can buy shoes that fit properly, don't pinch, blister, or otherwise torture your feet, and leave your back intact at the same time? If your man insists on four-inch heels, give him a pair for Christmas and tell him to dance the night away—I defy him to make it down the driveway in the suckers.

Accessible Accessories.   Put your belts, scarves, and others where you can see them. This could be a rack that displays them either within or outside of the closet, or it could be a series of drawers inside your closet that have special dividers (wide) so that they can be stored, yet accessible.

Happy Birthday, Dad.   Okay, pop, you've got ties coming out of your you-know-what. Maybe you're even a tie freak. What are you going to do with all these ties, since clearly you can only wear one at a time? Get the portable, install-it-yourself system that holds all the ties in the closet on individual pegs and slides out for easy viewing and selection.

Skirt around It.   Hang your skirts on skirt hangers that attach individually to each other to have either a layered or single-skirt effect. With these hangers, you can hang, for example, three black skirts in a layer and two white skirts in another layer, thus keeping everything organized by color and saving space at the same time. There are also special racks

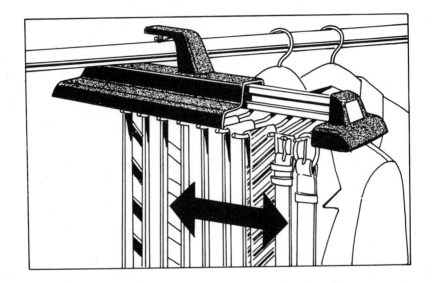

The rack above is great for keeping ties or belts orderly without taking up a lot of space. Attach the pants rack, at left and below, to the inside of your closet door to keep your slacks wrinkle free and accessible.

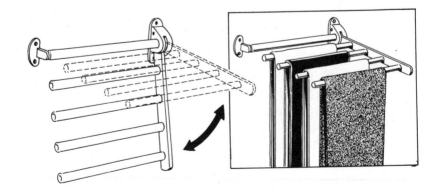

for pants that work on much the same idea. See the illustration on the opposite page.

Passé Plastic. When you bring in garments from the cleaners, get rid of the plastic covering. This stuff just collects dust, makes it hard for you to really see what you've got, and is dangerous for children and pets—they could suffocate. Tear it off immediately. Well, now I suppose some smart aleck is going to point out that the reason you *should* keep the plastic is *because* it collects dust, and hence the clothes stay dust-free. But if you've got something shrouded in plastic hanging in that closet of yours, and it has been there so long it's collecting dust, *why* is it hanging in your closet? Clothes are for wearing, not for collecting dust.

No Wire Hangers. Wire hangers are dreadful, and they should be replaced with good plastic hangers with a swivel head. They allow you to put the garment on the hanger any way you wish and still hang the clothing facing the same direction. Huh? Facing the same direction? That's right—believe it or not, facing the same direction saves space, and once you get into the habit of hanging your clothes all one way, with the aid of the swivel hangers, you'll find that you wouldn't have it any other way. I swear.

Double-Rod It. Installing a double-rod system immediately doubles your closet space, and that means you can hang pants and shirts or blouses and skirts in half the space you used before. It also means that you can color coordinate the outfits in hanging order. A double rod system is an improvement to your property; if you rent, you can look into the systems available that can be removed and taken with you when you leave. See page 140.

STOP AND SHOP

Whoopee, you finished! Now you get to go shopping, remember? Try to remember these shopping tips as you go:

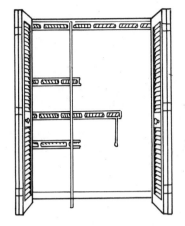

These are three examples of some different systems that can be installed to add more space in your existing closets.

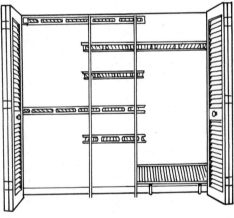

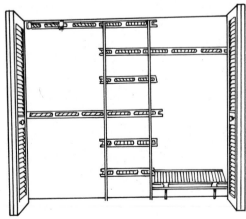

Closet Maid Storage Systems by Clairson International, Ocala, Florida.

Inventory. Make an inventory of what you already have. Then sit down and make a list of what you *need*—not what you *want*, but what you *need*.

Don't Leave Home without It. Your list—take it with you. Don't buy anything that isn't on the list, no matter what.

Take It with You. Take your favorite blouse or blazer with you. You can then buy pieces to work with it, and you can mix and match as you go.

Quality Counts. Classic, well-made garments are worth the price. You can wear them for years and always look and feel great.

It's on Sale! Don't, I repeat, don't, buy something just because it is on sale. If you don't need it, what difference does it make that it's on sale? Think about those clothes you just cleared out of your closet. If you never wore it, or it didn't go with anything, why did you buy it in the first place? Because it was on sale, of course. Try, if you can, to learn from your mistakes. In this case, it was and will be a mistake to buy useless garments just because they are on sale. I know you've done it, we've all done it, I'm just saying, don't do it anymore. On the other hand, if it's on sale, and it's on your list, snap it up, and take it home and brag your brains out to everyone within earshot about what a great bargain you got.

Shop Spring and Fall. We'll make an exception for this little spree, but in general, shop twice a year only. Depending on your pocketbook, this may mean that as soon as the fall fashions come out, you go out and do your shopping, and when the new summer styles come out, you do your spring and summer shopping. If your budget could use some trimming, you might still shop twice each year, except instead of running out to shop the minute the new fashions are presented, wait until they go on sale; then go out and make your purchases. Just before summer fashions are introduced, the winter things go on sale—that's the time to buy your winter things. And when the new winter styles are about to be presented, all the spring and summer things go on sale. That's the time to buy your summer things. Generally, if you shop wisely, you'll find that your clothing purchases won't be out of synch with the styles, partly because the fashion industry shows things well before we are ready for them. Winter things come out in July when it's hotter than blazes and go on sale sometime between November and January when you are freezing your watzit off, which makes sale time the time to buy for more reasons than one.

Cozy Up. Make friends with a salesperson who knows your taste in clothes, color preferences, and sizes. This can save you wads of time that might otherwise be wasted prowling the malls and department stores.

Complete It Please. Buy your accessories when you buy the outfit (if you don't already have them). You thus ensure a complete, pulled-together look that you can assemble at a moment's notice and without much effort or thought.

Color Me Pretty. Determine what your best colors are and then stick to that color palette. Try to keep it to four basic colors or less, and don't permit yourself to be suckered into buying something in this season's newest, faddiest color, when you know perfectly well that it is not one of the colors that look great on you. If your colors mix well, that only makes your possibilities extend themselves. For instance, I like red, white, black, beige. Occasionally I throw in a brown or a pink, and everything pretty much goes with everything else.

Consult a Consultant. A wardrobe or a color consultation with a professional can be well worth the money you spend. You'll be amazed at the special suggestions for your wardrobe, and you may find yourself changing or updating your image as a result, saving expensive mistakes at the same time.

OTHER CLOSETS

Seems like we've done the worst first here. And we really have, because not only does the disorder in our clothes closet drive us crazy when we try to find something reasonable to wear, that disorder is often reflected in the way we look. So doing those closets first can often give us, not only an organizational morale boost but a fashion boost as well.

THE LINEN CLOSET

Now, what about those other closets? You know—the hall closet and the linen closet. And what about the dreaded utility closet? Ouch.

Let's start with the easiest—the linen closet. The best thing you can do with a linen closet is to not have so darned many linens. Just because you *have* a linen closet doesn't mean you have to choke it with enough sheets, pillow cases, and towels for twenty people. You could consider assigning a small space on a shelf in each of the closets in your bedrooms. Put two sets of sheets (maximum) on that shelf. Then when you go to change the bed, the sheets that fit that bed are in the proper room and you don't have to dig through a big pile in your linen closet. You can use the same method with towels, particularly if you have nice ones. (You should have *some* nice ones!) You can install a Lucite shelf or two in the bathroom—maybe over the commode—fold your towels and washcloths nicely, and put them on the shelf. When you have guests, they can help themselves to clean towels, and the rest of the family doesn't have to make periodic mad nude dashes to the linen closet when they get out of the shower dripping wet and realize there's no clean towel available.

THE UTILITY CLOSET

The utility closet presents special problems. It too, can best be managed by getting all the junk out of there, leaving just the basics behind (broom, dustpan, mop, etc.). And yes, if you don't have any place to put the twenty-five-pound bag of dog food, or the bag of cat litter, you *can* also store those items in the utility closet. If this applies to you (and even if it doesn't) you might find it handy to buy some of the utility clamp hooks and strips that you can install inside the closet to hang your broom and mop, clearing space on the floor for your other no-place-to-put-it items.

THE HALL CLOSET

And what about one of the most gruesome closets in the house—the hall or the spare closet. I was once interviewed by a radio station, and the final question I was asked was, "Well, Stephanie Culp, what's in *your* hall closet?" Uh oh.

Here is what was in my hall closet on that day:

AIRLINE CAT KENNEL

TRUNK (with nothing in it)

A BUNCH OF BOOKS

SUITCASE

COATS, JACKETS, SWEATERS

BUSINESS MATERIALS IN BINDERS (I hadn't looked at them in years!)

VACUUM CLEANER

TWO UMBRELLAS

THREE CANVAS BAGS WITH STUPID SAYINGS ON THEM

CLOTHES FOR CHARITY

A ROLL OF UPHOLSTERY FABRIC

ARCHITECTURAL PLANS

ROLL OF WALLPAPER

TWO THROW RUGS

TWO AMUSING THROW PILLOWS

BOOTS THAT I NEVER WEAR

WRAPPING PAPER (all scrunched up by now, as you can well imagine)

And my hall closet is very *small*. Needless to say, I went home that evening and cleaned it out!

Cleaning out the hall closet is simple: Throw out as much stuff as you can (or give it to charity). Lots of what was in my hall closet bit the dust, believe me. As with everything else, if you're not using it, and can get along very well without it, why are you storing it? I ask my clients that question constantly. On that dark night I had to ask *myself* that question. To help myself get rid of a goodly portion of what had amassed, I took the acid test—I asked myself if I would want to pay to move it (each item), since I was thinking about moving. That made me think of one of my favorite clients and her penchant for keeping absolutely everything. Her pack-rat tendencies, along with her other eccentricities, all came to a head the day she decided to move out of state. Of course she called me to organize the move.

NEXT TO HER, YOU LOOK GREAT

Her idea of moving was a bit different than most. She began by going out and actually *buying* outright a used truck, moving-van size, and parking it, with a flourish, in her driveway. She had to be out in two weeks, because she was having a dispute of world war proportions with the owner of the house and, while she could have afforded to buy ten houses herself, in this particular instance she was renting. The dispute culminated in an eviction proceeding with lawyers all over the place (and now this truck in the driveway and a fourteen-day time limit in which to pack her up). In fourteen days, at midnight supposedly, the marshals were coming. I could hardly wait.

She had a two-bedroom house—not that large, really—but considering what awaited behind closet doors, I knew fourteen days would just barely do it.

I had to hire one guy to just stand there and wash hangers because she insisted that everything be washed, and this included hangers (she had hundreds of them). I hired packers with packing experience so she'd be satisfied with how her belongings were packed. I hired an artist to tape the boxes shut, because she insisted that the tape end at exactly the same place on each box. All the boxes had to have the same color print on them—green, I think it was. I had one guy, the Supply Sergeant, who did nothing but go and get the proper supplies (this meant only supplies that would make this client happy—not an easy task) and bring us food. When he wasn't chasing around for supplies and meals, he was disconnecting her audio equipment, which was a job in itself. I hired one woman to just fold and pack her mountains of clothes ever so perfectly in tissue paper. Everyone worked ten to fourteen hours each day for two weeks.

During this whole process my client had managed to gather up a hefty cache of things that were "vital" and "could not be packed." On the final day, with four hours to go, I estimated that there were at least ten cartons worth of stuff, plus a carload of personal items, yet to be packed. She had hoarded these goodies for fourteen days, and now she refused to budge.

With two hours to go, the driver of the truck (a friend of hers she'd recruited for the job) announced emphatically that at five minutes before the magic hour of twelve, he intended to drive that truck up the hill and out the gate, he didn't care what. Finally, with one hour to go, and everybody bone tired, my people threatening to walk off the job and go home, she said we could pack the rest of it up. Mind you, that meant loading a goodly portion of it up into her car. Her car, Geronimo (that was the car's name—she named her cars), was parked down the hill at the back gate. By now, the concrete steps leading out the back gate had been ripped out and the outside lights removed (these were all improvements she had made to the property and she certainly was not going to leave them to that blankety-blank landlord who was sending over the marshals). So we caravanned down that dark hill like a bunch of lunatics in the bush, burdened with loads of stuff for Geronimo.

At exactly five minutes before twelve, the driver hopped into the truck and revved it up. The truck groaned a little (it was packed solid) before it pulled victoriously up the hill and out the gate. We loaded the stuff designated for the dump (mostly construction materials from the ripped-out improvements) into another truck that was standing by, packed my client into Geronimo, wished her happy trails, and skeedaddled out of there.

As you square off with your closets, you might want to remember to put yourself to the acid test—is it worth moving? Would someone else love it and use it much more than you? Are you using or wearing it? Does it need time-consuming special care? Test yourself on each closet—in the end you'll probably come out at the head of the class, and your many belongings will be out of the closet and organized for good.

Twelve

'

Papernoia

Computers are here, it appears, for good. We're on our way to the "paperless" society. That's what I keep hearing, anyway. The problem with that statement is that whoever said it has obviously never received much mail.

I often sit down just to contemplate and wonder. And while I'm about this contemplating and wondering, I wonder why it is that when I was eighteen, I got very little if any mail and didn't care one whit about the mail. If I didn't get any mail at all for weeks at a time, it didn't bother me in the least. I was eighteen, and had other, more important, things on my mind. Like leaving home and boys for instance. Now, at thirty-nine, I get tons of mail, and its arrival has taken on a level of importance that magically increases with age. Since a substantial portion of the mail I receive has to do with unpleasant things like unpaid bills, it doesn't make sense to me that the mail should be something that I would even *want* to look at, much less organize. Still, it's The Mail. And sooner or later, one has to deal with the paper-processing problems that come marching right in the door under the pseudonym "mail."

The mail often includes not only the bills but invitations (usually to weddings or parties that require gifts), solicitations, personal notes, junk mail, and magazines and catalogs. And that's just the mail that comes to your *house*. If you have a job that requires attention to paperwork, then you are really a candidate for Paper Problems. Whether you open your mail at home or at work—or both, in which case, you've got a paper double whammy on your hands—and whether you operate from a home-based business or a corporate office, paper, believe me, is here to stay.

The computer people keep telling us that paper is going to go away, and, I don't know, maybe it is, but before that really happens, the paper that is piling up all around you needs to be processed before the electricity gets turned off, or your Aunt Thelma decides never to speak to you again because you never answer her letters, you stupid ingrate.

The constant barrage of paper can be awesome. So awesome, in fact, that it can be difficult to find the time to figure out how to manage the paper problem, let alone actually *do* something with all that paper. If you haven't taken care of yesterday's, or last week's, mail, there is no way you are going to have time to take care of the paper that gets dumped on you today. If you are being inundated with paper and you don't have the time, or the know-how, to bring the paper problem under control, then you are probably suffering from papernoia. Papernoics get a little freaked out once the paper gets out of control and is piled up all over the place. Eventually, things get so piled up, lost, and behind that "disorganized" is one of the more polite terms you hear aimed in the general direction of the harried sufferer. Finally, things slowly grind to a halt, and your secretary starts thinking about checking out the rates at the funny farm—and maybe she's checking on a few rates for herself, not just for you. Because papernoics drive everyone around them crazy as they consistently forget, lose, and otherwise hopelessly mismanage their mail and paper flow.

But there's hope. The news on the medical front is that papernoia can be avoided and time saved if the patient can just manage to grasp a few basic principles about paper.

The first principle is to accept the fact that if you don't do anything else with the papers, at least you should *sort* the incoming proliferation. Then, if and when you decide to actually *do* something *about* all that paperwork, at least it is organized and waiting happily for you to work on it in your usual systematic, efficient, *organized,* manner.

THE FOUR KINDS OF PAPERS

There are essentially only four things to be done with paper. Set up these four baskets:

TO DO

TO PAY

TO FILE

TO READ

Then, of course, there's the trash basket. Put your "to do" basket and your "to pay" basket on top of your desk. The best baskets are the wire ones that can be stacked. You can see into them so you always know how much work is there, and there's plenty of room for your fat little hand to reach in and grab the papers. Fancy smoke-colored boxes that, when stacked, are impossible to work with easily are paper traps. Get rid of them if you have them and go back to the wire ones. It's generally best to have the "to do" basket on top, and the "to pay" basket on the bottom.

For your "to read," get a sturdy *large* wicker basket

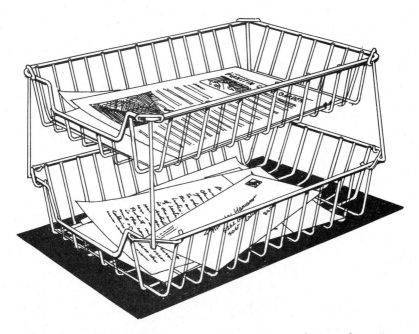

Wire baskets make it easy for you to see at a glance what you have "to do" and "to pay."

with a handle. This can be kept anywhere—on the floor in the bedroom, in the bathroom, on the floor behind your desk, on the credenza, whatever. And it's portable—you can carry it from place to place.

For your "to file" category, get a really roomy wicker basket and put it *under* your desk. You don't need all that filing on top of your desk getting in the way of important "to do" and "to pay" matters.

Remember that sorting your mail into those four categories doesn't mean that you have "to do" it, or "to pay" it, or even "to file" it immediately; you merely sort it in order to do whatever it is you are supposed to do with it later. *Future timesaver:* Next time you need to find something, you won't have to go through every piece of paper; you will only have to go through the pile in the appropriate category. For instance, if you have a bill collector on the phone and you need to lay your hands on that unpaid bill (of course, we know you *intend* to pay it, you just haven't done so *yet*), all you have to do is search through the "to pay" pile, and presto, you will find it in one-fourth the time it would have taken you to look for it if you had had to search through all the papers.

Remember too that once you throw something away, you aren't going to have a pile to search through. That is, unless you thought you could start a pile of "to toss" papers, in which case, go to jail, and do *not* pass Go. Toss means trash can, and once something hits that can, it should not be reclaimed for any reason—the trash can is *not* a filing cabinet or holding center for your indecisions.

Make sure your "to file" basket is roomy enough to collect lots of your "to be filed" papers.

MOVE THAT PAPER

Okay, now you have the sorting concept firmly in mind, and you vow to *sort* from this day forth. Try some of these ideas to help you handle your mail and paperwork in a more organized fashion:

Open Up. Open and sort your mail as soon as you get it. Throw away all the junk inserts, then sort the mail into our categories, "to do," "to pay," "to file," and "to read."

Use a Letter Opener. If you have already balked at the "open the mail right away" part, go out and buy yourself a fancy letter opener to help you accomplish the dirty deed. Letter openers are fun, sexy, and efficient. Maybe if you get yourself one, you'll trick yourself into using it to actually open the mail promptly.

Junk the Junk. Scan the junk mail right then and there (if you are interested in it in the first place) and then do what you should be doing with junk—throw it away. Why do you think they call it junk mail?

Circular File. Place a *roomy* trash basket next to, or under, your desk. Dinky, fancy trash cans have no business in an office or work area. One day's junk mail alone could topple such a boudoir basket. Use your large trash basket regularly and generously—after all, some things were clearly destined to become trash from the outset.

To Do It. Have a roomy "to do" basket. Everything that requires some kind of action goes into this box. This does *not* mean that you have "to do" it that minute; it merely means that you intend to do it soon, and you *will*.

To ensure that you don't let your "to do" box become a burial ground, start each day by going through the box and prioritizing what needs to be done. If some of the projects are long-term ones, and especially if you find yourself procrastinating repeatedly by not *doing* those particular projects in your box, you might have to sit down and pencil in on your calendar exactly when you are going to spend the time on that project in your "to do" box that you have, up to now, been avoiding. Then, when that day rolls around, you will know that you are going to put other matters aside so that you can give that particular project your attention.

Forget Pending. Beware of "pending" files. Too often a category for "pending" is established only to have items placed within become either lost or happily forgotten forever. Something you think of as "pending" is actually something that needs to be done sooner or later. Therefore, it too goes in the "to do" box, where it won't be forgotten, since you'll see it every time you work on the papers in that box.

Buy Now, Pay Later. Have a "to pay" basket and put all due bills and bank statements into it. Once a month (or, when and/or *if* you get the necessary money), simply take care of all of your financial and bookkeeping obligations in one sitting. In the meantime, if you need to check a current (or not-so-current) bill, you'll know exactly where you put it.

Balance. Keep your checkbook balanced, even if it means having a bookkeeper do it for you each month. Remember, however, in order for the bookkeeper to do this, you must be a good do-bee and note on your check register the amount of the check written and to whom it was written. Putting that chore off, even for a few minutes, is an open invitation to disaster.

ABC It. Some things get filed. All right, *lots* of things get filed. Leaving papers that need to be filed on top of your desk or dining room table only adds to the clutter and the confusion. One solution is to get a large shallow basket, and put it on the floor near, or under, your desk or worktable. (I use the kind small pets sleep in.) This is now your "to file" basket. Everything that needs to be filed goes into it until you have time to do the filing (or better yet, until you have someone else do it for you). Filing, yuck.

Pendaflex Your Files. Use a Pendaflex filing system. It is the most functional kind on the market. Remember to put the plastic tabs on the *front* of the Pendaflex jacket, not the back. This way, when your finger touches the already very visible tab, you automatically pull the file jacket open so that you can grab the manila folder inside quickly and easily.

Don't Overstuff. Don't overstuff any particular file. You will only choke up your filing system and make papers hard to retrieve. When a file starts to get full, make another one; break the second one down by date or another pertinent fact. For example, "Correspondence, Jane Doe, Jan-June 1986" and "Correspondence Jane Doe, July-December 1986."

To File or Not to File. Remember that fully 80 percent of all papers filed are never looked at again. Save yourself some filing time and remember that, the next time you want to file some obscure article or piece of correspondence that you really don't need to keep.

Out in the Open. Never keep any work in progress inside your desk drawers. See to it that people who work for you abide by this rule as well. All work in progress should go into the "to do" or "to pay" baskets, and nowhere else! Thus work not yet finished won't become buried (and therefore lost) in a drawer somewhere. At the same time, you will be able to tell at a glance the amount of work yet to be done or the status of work currently in progress.

Ongoing Projects. If you frequently work on projects that result in lots of bulky papers (e.g., if you are a writer or an attorney, or a student with several assignments), you may have to assign an area other than the "to do" basket for the bulk. A credenza, bookcase, or table behind your desk can serve as the staging/holding area for these projects, so long as they are neatly and categorically stacked. Another way to hold such papers is to get a rolling cart for the temporary project, which you can break down (if you like) in files. When the project is completed, simply transfer the files to transfile boxes for storage, and set the cart up with whatever new project you might have underway.

What's Today's Date? Keep a calendar on your desk near the telephone so that you can easily refer to it for your scheduling needs. Note any last-minute changes as they occur, and if you have a secretary, see to it that he uses and refers to your calendar as well. Carry some kind of calendar with you, even if it's only a tiny card on your checkbook.

Number Please. Keep your phone numbers on a Rolodex that's large enough to accommodate your needs. As you collect phone numbers (from business cards or tiny scraps

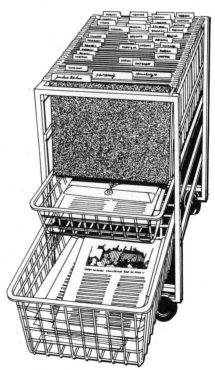

This rolling cart is great for special projects. If you've got children, let them each have their own cart, so that they can "file" their school papers when they bring them home. Their art projects fit nicely in the baskets underneath.

of papers with numbers hastily scribbled on them), throw them into a small basket or container. Periodically, you (or someone else) can sit down and type up the cards for the Rolodex. *Future timesaver:* Once again, if, before these numbers get typed up, you need to scrounge up a number on a moment's notice, you'll know it isn't lost. It's either *on* the Rolodex already, *or* it's in the basket waiting to be typed and put onto the Rolodex. This little tip can do wonders for your professional life, and it might just perk up your social life as well!

May I Take a Message?   Keep a pen or pencil and note pad by every telephone so that you or anyone who answers the phone can easily take a message, thus eliminating missed calls and messages.

Message Center.   Establish a message center where all messages can be dropped. This can be a bulletin board, basket, or bin, or whatever works in your environment. Then ask everyone to drop the messages there, and it becomes a simple matter for one and all to check the message center on their way in or out of the house or office.

Quick, Grab a Pen.   Keep all your pens and pencils on top of your desk in one large container—the simpler, the better. A glass jar that lets you see your selection clearly is better than some fancy opaque gizmo that you have to dig around in to find your favorite pen.

Another One Bites the Dust.   While you are digging around for pens, the next time you pull one out and find it doesn't write, *don't put it back. Throw it away!!!*

Buy Stamps by the Roll.   Constantly running out of stamps is a lame excuse for not getting things out in the mail on time. Buy stamps by the roll, and see to it that you buy more before you totally run out. If you don't like standing in line at the post office (oh, c'mon, you mean you don't *enjoy* waiting in line so you can be treated like a peasant by some surly postal clerk—where's your sense of humor?), order your stamps by mail and *in advance.*

Traveling Correspondence. Carry your notebook or postcards with you so that you can use waiting time (in the doctor's office, at the airport, at the hairdresser) to catch up on some of your personal correspondence.

Paper Relatives. Besides the notebook or postcards you carry with you, consider fitting fifteen minutes into your schedule each day to write one personal note or letter to a friend or relative. You can do it over your morning coffee, or in the evening while you watch television. It's only fifteen minutes of your day, and it adds up to seven letters per week or thirty pieces of correspondence handled per month. Of course, if you're the type of person who loves to run off at the mouth on paper and can't possibly write a letter in fifteen minutes, try instead to set aside an hour a week (perhaps on Monday evening) to write letters and keep up with your personal correspondence. The return in the quality of relationships with your personal correspondents will be almost immeasurable.

Traveling Companion. Treat your briefcase just as you do your work area—with the four-step paper-sorting process. Make files titled "to do," "to pay," "to file," and "to read." As materials accumulate that for one reason or another are going to be transported by briefcase, instead of throwing the papers in a pile into the case, put them in the appropriate file. You'll be able to deal with the material in a more organized manner, and the chances of something getting lost or misplaced are reduced. Also be sure to keep some essentials in your briefcase: a box of paper clips, several pens, a small stapler, small scissors, and some Scotch tape. This way, whether you are on the commuter train or leaving home to go directly to a client's office, you can organize your paperwork as easily as if you were at your desk. Here's another quick tip for your briefcase: I've added one more folder to my case—"Xerox."

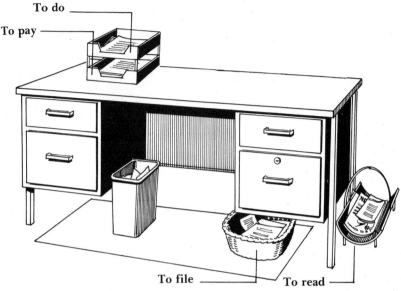

Use the four-step paper system to sort your papers as they come in. By doing this, you'll avoid having piles of papers everywhere. Remember you make life much easier for yourself if you move a two-drawer filing cabinet right next to your desk. This way, you can pull files and refile without even getting out of your chair.

I'm always running off to the copy shop to get something copied, so now I just drop the papers to be copied in that file as they accumulate, and as I pass the shop, I dash in with them. When I get the copies, I sort them right then into the files in my briefcase as they are handed back to me. Some of them are "to do" (mail out, perhaps), many are "to file," and some are "to pay" or even "to read." When I return to my office, it is a simple matter to transfer the materials in those briefcase files into the proper baskets at my work station.

Tidy Up. Spend ten to fifteen minutes at the end of each day tidying up your work area. It helps to clear your head a bit when you put everything in its place once each day. When you start on your mail or paperwork the following day, you will feel that you are making a fresh start on your work and the day.

Thirteen

Car Crazy

Organize my car? Are you crazy? The car doesn't "get organized"! Wanna bet? Besides the trash you've accumulated on the floor and under the seat, the glove compartment stuffed to the gills with God knows what, and the contents of the trunk (you try not to open the trunk if possible, you just know that the junk back there is rolling around and making weird noises from time to time)—besides all that, consider these possibilities brought to you from real life experience.

Ever had your radiator fall out of, yes, *fall out* of, your El Dorado at the top of Laurel Canyon? For those of you who have somehow missed the experience, here's what happens: the car goes berserk and has a total nervous breakdown. Buzzers go, lights blink hysterically, and bells ding from every conceivable direction. Once you miraculously have rolled down the hill, rounded up a tow to the nearest mechanic, and, once there, hauled out your checkbook, you find, amidst lots of clucking and tsk-tsking, that apparently the *last* mechanic who worked on the radiator forgot to put the bolts back in the radiator, and now you get to take the bus home because it's too late to fix the car. And once it does get fixed, the cost of the repair will put you on a diet of bread and water for months.

Or, how about the time your European guest took your Honda for a quick spin down to the local Ralph's supermarket for some bread and cat food. Exiting, nearly comatose from the Ralph's experience, she wraps the front fender, bumper, and assorted underneath stuff around a pole in the parking lot. Read one frame job and some tires. (You'll live with the dents in the bumper for now.)

And when was the last time you took the car in for a tune-up and it turned into a valve job? For those of you not familiar with a valve job, have patience. Trust me—sooner or later, nearly everyone hears the dreaded words, "valve job." When it happens to you, run straight to the cardiologist. We are talking big money here, my friend, and guaranteed, it'll give you a heart attack when you get the news.

What else can go wrong? Oh, just about everything. Like the transmission, for instance. Or the generator, or the alternator, or any of those other miscellaneous doodads located under the hood. And brakes. You gotta have brakes, and brakes *always* go, sooner or later.

Part of owning a car is the problem of maintenance and repairs. Oh, I know when you buy the car for a zillion dollars, you think that it will never break down, but of course it does. And when you are talking car trouble, you're talking nervous breakdown at best, and at worst, outright murder. Me, I have my nervous breakdown right away and get it over with. Because the mechanics don't care. Tears, pleading poverty, begging for mercy; none of this works with them. They know you *need*, you *gotta have* your wheels, and furthermore, you mean no later than tomorrow. And they're right.

Because without the car (unless you live in a city and take the subway) you're doomed. Talk about time management. No car can mean throwing your schedule right out the window. It does take significantly more time to *walk* than it does to drive or ride to your destination. When the car goes, all but the most necessary events are canceled. You somehow figure out how to get to the store and to work. Period. No shopping, socializing, galavanting, or fast-tracking, without ye olde automobile.

You're stuck with alternate means of transportation, which generally means you beg someone to bail you out and give you a lift here and there. While some big cities have decent transportation, many do not. In lots of cities, if you've got all the time in the world, you just might be able to get to where you're going on one of the buses; then again, there's a good chance that there's no bus route anywhere near either your home or your destination.

Besides the fact that alternate transportation may be nonexistent, it takes *time*. You don't have time to waste, so it's critical that you establish an organized relationship with your car. In return, your car will do its level best to get you where you are going on time.

So, from the point of purchase, how do you organize the care and feeding of your car? This purchase may cost you, in dollars and cents, a lot more than your kids do, and it will give you about the same treatment before it dies for good. The one big difference between the car and the kids is that you can trade in the car when you get sick of it, and you get no such option with the kids. But before the car goes for good, here are some ways to keep things organized in your efforts to keep the car running past the life of the payment plan.

KEEP YOUR CAR IN THE PRIME OF LIFE

Fill Er Up!   Don't let the gas tank reach empty before you refill it. It's bad for the car, and besides, what happens if there's a disaster? Like an earthquake, for example. You have to get out of the disaster zone, traffic is tied up for thirty miles, and you don't have enough gas to idle in the ensuing traffic jam for more then ten frustrating minutes. Or suppose you have to transport an injured person or pet to the hospital in an emergency situation? You won't be in the mood to stop for gas should that happen, I can assure you.

Spare Me. Always keep an inflated spare tire. This sounds simple enough, but consider this: you get a flat, replace it with the spare, and throw the dud tire back into the trunk. Three months later you get another flat (c'mon, have you been rotating your tires, like a good do-bee?), and what are you going to change that dud tire with? You forgot to get the other one fixed or replaced, and what was an inconvenience and expense three months ago has now become a *major* problem and expense, involving lots of money and time and maybe even a tow.

Instant Tires. If you trot on down to the place in your area that sells all the car parts and gizmos, you will find, among other things, some instant inflate-your-tires stuff. It comes in a can. Get yourself some, because I'm here to tell you that it works, it really does. And when you have a slow leak or a flat tire and no spare because you didn't get a spare like I told you to, this canned stuff will inflate your tire (in most, but not all, cases—blowouts are beyond help) and get you going far enough to buy another tire.

Safety First. Be sure to keep safety basics in the car. These include flares, flashlight, map, blanket, tire-changing tools, water, and a "Call Police" sign. All these items could come in handy and maybe even save your life late at night on a dark, unfamiliar road.

Join the Club. Join an auto club. Auto clubs will do everything from tow you to get you back into the car after you have absent-mindedly locked yourself out of it. They change tires, give you gas when you run out, and provide travel-information services. They even, in some cases, post bail for you if you are thrown into the hoosegow for a traffic violation.

Auto clubs are worth the money they charge, not only for the peace of mind they give you but also for the time you will save. Try walking to the nearest station to get help instead of making a phone call from a call box or telephone the next time you break down. Day or night, you can call the auto club, and the time you save in the end is almost impossible to measure accurately.

Tune Her Up. Follow a regular maintenance schedule. This means that you should tune up the car when the manual says to tune it up. If the manual says to have the brakes checked at 20,000 miles, then have the brakes checked. If you don't do as you're told by the manual (you *can* read, can't you?), you may invalidate your warranty, and the car will probably break down on you sooner that it would have had you done what you were supposed to do. Remember, when you turn the car in to the repair shop, you might as well turn in your perfectly organized schedule with it.

Change the Oil. Your car also needs to have the oil changed even more often that the regular tune-up. So, every couple of thousand miles, make a note, and change the oil and maybe the filter. About the filter: every now and then when you have the car serviced, if you've asked for a new oil filter along with an oil change, do yourself a favor, and *look* at the filter to see if the mechanic really changed the darned thing. I found out about this one the hard way: when my old car reached the valve-job stage, I was curtly informed that the old filter looked as if it had never been changed—it was a mess. Upon inspection, it did appear that the mechanic was right— the thing had probably never been changed—and this in spite of the fact that I had paid for that "change" many times over.

Rotate the Tires. This is like the oil and the oil filter. You need to have it done regularly, and you might want to consider getting sneaky about getting it done. I marked a tire once, took the car in, and told the mechanic, among other things, to rotate the tires. He said he'd done it, and he certainly charged me for it, but my little mark was still there, on the same tire, which was in the same spot on the car. The fact is, he did *not* rotate those tires. Rotation helps ensure that the tires last longer, save you money and time, and provides a safer vehicle for you to drive.

Baby, It's Hot in Here.   Probably so, because once again you forgot to have the maintenance people check out the air-conditioning system the last time the car was in the shop. If you are like most people, you wait until it breaks down before you check it, and of course, then it's too late. The air conditioning invariably breaks down during the hottest, busiest month of the year. You can't possibly take the time to be without a car to get the a/c fixed, and so you swelter in the heat. Remember that you, too, can avoid that slow burn by simply giving the a/c system a quick once-over every now and then.

Just Fix It, Please.   Get a good mechanic. When your car breaks down, what you really need is a miracle. And in the auto-repair field, a miracle translates into a person who's not out to take every cent you have and who'll do a good, conscientious job, as quickly and reasonably as possible. Think about it. Your car never breaks down in front of your house, and wherever it breaks down, you're going to need a reliable mechanic so that you can tell the tow-truck driver where to go. (I love tow-truck drivers. They're like birds. Vultures, that is. My car was once towed because it was parked illegally—it wasn't my fault, I loaned it to a friend who parked it illegally—and I had to redeem my car late on a Saturday night. Cash was the only acceptable form of payment the kidnappers would take for ransom, and because it was a Saturday night, I was reduced to rolling pennies from the humongous water bottle that I toss pennies into. Finally I assembled the required sixty-five dollars, borrowed the neighbor's car, and went to bail out my car. "You know," I told the man counting my pennies, "I have managed to live thirty-seven years without this particular experience, and I want to take this opportunity to tell you that I would have preferred to live another thirty-seven years without going through this." "Well," he drawled, counting the money, "a body has to experience the bad things in life, in order to appreciate the good things that come their way." What a guy.) If you find a good mechanic early, *before* you have major breakdown problems, when the tow truck shows up, you can, as I said, tell the driver where to go. Use your mechanic for all your minor maintenance and get to know him or her on a first-name basis. (Forget about this for tow-truck drivers.) If your mechanic is at a gas station, buy all your gas there. Smile. Be nice. Be polite and patient. Later, you'll be glad you did, believe me.

No Deal. When it comes to repairs, going back to your dealer is not necessarily the answer. The repair department at the car dealership where you bought the car will have you believe that they are the only ones on earth who can service your car properly. Don't you believe it. It is almost a certainty that they will *charge* more than anyone else, but it is a myth that they are the only people who can repair your Ford or Toyota. So don't automatically head for the dealer, especially if you are on a budget. There are mechanics who specialize in repairs on different car makes; you just need to find them *before* the car breaks down. You'll save gobs of time for yourself later on.

Opinionated. On major repair work, get a second opinion. Don't let the first mechanic you talk with convince you that your car needs an organ transplant of major proportions until you've talked to another mechanic and confirmed the diagnosis.

CAR PAPERWORK

Besides keeping your car operating, you have to keep up on its ownership. This requires some attention to paperwork.

Insure It. Insure it to the hilt. Take it from me. I've been totaled. The car got last rites on the spot, but if it hadn't been for the fact that I had a good policy on what was, essentially, a pretty junky car, I'd have been in big trouble. I was sued, and I wound up seeing doctors for well over a year. My insurance company took care of it all. And if you think you'll never have an accident, think again. I was pulling out of my driveway and got slammed into on the driver's side. The person who hit me also hit a telephone pole, and eight months later I got a bill from the telephone company for the scratch on the pole. My insurance company paid for that too, and gave me just enough money for a down payment on another car. So bite the bullet, and get insured. Of course the rates are outrageous and an insult to mankind. But in spite of that, in the case of my particular accident, I have to say they took care of things. You should have seen the doctor's bills, the lawsuit, and the bill from the telephone company. (Of course, I've got a few things I could say about doctors, lawyers, and the telephone company too.)

Have the Number in the Car. Always carry the name and number of your insurance agent with you in the car. You never know when you'll need it. In my case, I was able to hobble back upstairs to my apartment to call my agent. I was in shock, and because of this, stupidly let the other party, who was less injured than I, use my phone. She called her lawyer and they sued *me*.

Registration. Always keep your registration in the car with you, and keep a copy in your files. I know you are a perfect driver, but chances are the highway patrol hasn't figured that out yet, and when a cop stops you for doing something stupid, he or she always wants to see the registration.

Traveling Sales. If your work means that you are in your car a great deal of the time, servicing or selling to customers, then you will need to somehow accommodate some supplies in the car. Get a tackle box and put what you need inside—paper clips, stapler, pens, business cards, rubber bands, Post-It pads, etc. It will serve you in the car as well as in your home, the office, and the client's location. The box ensures that your traveling business will go a little more smoothly than if you had to wait until you returned to the office, or if you are reduced to stuffing the glove compartment and console with supply odds and ends.

Step into My Office.   Remember that the car is not really your office. It is easy to think this ignorant thought and as a consequence, leave papers in the car. Although it's easy to do, it's not so easy to find a particular piece of paper once you have tossed all those papers, with wild abandon, into the backseat. Where is that one document now? Under the seat? In that cute little overflowing plastic trash holder with the happy face on it? Did someone sit on it? Spill coffee on it? Uh oh. This is definitely gonna take some *time*.

Pay Up.   If you are making car payments, pretend to yourself that they are as important as the rent or the mortgage, and pay on time. Car-payment people exhibit remarkably little patience with chronic lateness or forgetfulness. Remember that if you are on time, you will get to keep the car, which will get you everywhere else on time.

Time to Renew.   At least a month before your car license plates reach their expiration date, mark your calendar "car registration due." Do this so that it doesn't sneak up on you, and you don't have the money or forget to send it in. Tags that are not current translate into immediate revenue for the city in the form of tickets to you.

New Mug Shot.   Plan well in advance (at least six to eight weeks) for driver's license renewal. If you live in a big city, chances are this process will take you one full day of standing in line at the very least. Not only will an expired driver's license get an ugly response from that cop who stops you, it will mean a costlier ticket, and time spent taking care of it.

And when you show that expired driver's license for identification at the supermarket or department store to back up your perfectly good check, you may be scornfully turned away like a common criminal.

Lock Down! You say you've locked yourself out of the car more than you'd care to remember? The next time, instead of having to wait for the auto club to come and bail you out, reach into your wallet and pull out that extra car key that you have cleverly put there for just such an emergency. This tip came to me from a woman who overheard me calling the auto club from a parking lot where I had just locked myself out of my car for the third time in six months.

I suppose the fact that *I*, the professional organizer, locked myself out of my car three times in six months has some of you snickering, and mumbling relievedly, "I knew it, I just knew it." You're right, of course. I am sometimes like the gardener with the concrete back yard. I don't follow my own advice all the time, and guess what, I get disorganized. But of course, just like everyone else, I can always come up with an *excuse*. In the case of the car and getting locked out, there's always, "I was in a rush," or "I had so many things on my mind," or "the parking attendant was so rude, he distracted me." But in this case, I did listen to the tip the woman gave me, and now I don't need excuses.

Now, I just whip out my extra key, let myself in the car where the other keys are gleaming from their comfy spot in the ignition, return the spare key to my wallet, and drive off. This saves time and frustration every single time.

Safety for Women Drivers. Unfortunately it is a fact that occasionally when a woman is driving alone and her car breaks down, an offer of help can come from a stranger who, after gaining access to the car and driver, proceeds to molest, rape, and sometimes even murder that woman driver. Of course there are genuine Good Samaritans out there, but most highway patrol officials suggest that women drivers whose cars break down should roll up the windows, lock the doors, and *not* accept help from passersby. This is particularly true on highways and freeways. You can purchase a sign that says PLEASE CALL POLICE; when not in use, it folds to fit in your glove compartment. In case of a breakdown, simply unfold the sign and put it in the back window of the car. Someone will undoubtedly call the police or highway patrol, and in the meantime, the sign will help deter potential hooligans.

KEEP IT NEAT

Here are some ways to keep your car from looking like a traveling trash bin.

Did You Say Gloves?   Use your glove compartment for things like your auto-club card, a penlight, pen, paper, local map, sunglasses, and your auto registration. Don't use that compartment for your lip gloss (the sun will make a mess you won't soon forget), your birth certificate, and the hammer.

Keep the Change.   Put change for parking meters or tolls in the console and keep it there. Nothing is more frustrating than finding a parking spot and then not having money for the meter. Or, how about when you don't have enough change for the amount of time you'll need, and Mary Meter Maid beats you to the car by a mere thirty seconds with her big fat ticket book, from which she writes you a big fat ticket?

If you don't have a recession in your console, get a plastic container of some sort and put change and toll tokens in it. If you can, glue or in some way attach the container to the dash, so you always have it within reach. If this isn't possible, get a container with a lid so that at least the lid will ensure that the money stays put and can be retrieved when necessary.

Dump City.   Don't use your trunk as a dumping ground. It should hold your safety tools, the spare tire, the blanket, and, if you insist, your gym clothes (phew!). You will thus have ample room for the groceries and the laundry, when you need to transport those types of things. Just because you have that little bit of room at your disposal doesn't mean that you should use the trunk as a permanent mobile storage unit. It will only make noises that you will mistake for car trouble, make it easier for you to "lose" things (after all, once the trunk is closed, who thinks about what's actually in there?), and you will only have another problem when you suddenly need to transport something (like the groceries) and there's no place to put anything in the trunk.

Cleanliness Is Next to Godliness.   Wash the car regularly. It gets gooky otherwise, and I am pretty positive that gooky cannot be good for a car. Bird-doo can't be especially helpful to the finish either, so don't let it accumulate along with the dirt, dust, and pollution residue. If you're ever gonna sell that baby (that is, assuming you ever pay it off, which is another sad story altogether), then you're going to want the finish to look nice. This means wash and wax, and if you don't want to handle the hose and chamois yourself, take it to a car-wash-and-wax place, or get the kid down the street to do it (or what about the kid in your own household—a little soap and water along with an hour of hard work never killed anybody).

Designer Seats.   Unless you've got easy-clean vinyl upholstery, sooner or later, your upholstery is going to be blessed with a messy spill. It might be coffee, but then again it could be dog throw-up. There's no way to escape it—the car upholstery gets dirty, yucky, and funky. Unless, of course, you take care of it. This means cleaning up the dog barf the instant it happens, not only getting rid of the barf, but also applying cleaner that works well on your particular upholstery. Any homemaker can tell you that this prevents the "stain from setting," and that translates to upping your chances of keeping the car interior looking nicer, longer. So besides the paper towels, which are great for blotting up messes, keep some upholstery cleaner in the trunk and apply it when necessary.

Clean That Up!   Also keep a roll of paper towels in the trunk. Paper towels can do duty as window wipers, napkins, and spill-wiper-uppers.

Tweet Tweet.   Keep a plastic lemon (the kind you get at the supermarket with lemon juice in it) filled with window cleaner in the glove compartment or trunk. When you find your window covered with lots of little bird surprises, you can whip out your lemon and clean the window before you take off from wherever it is you and the birdies are. Of course, if you keep your automatic window washer filled, you won't have to bother with plastic lemons.

I Can't See a Blankety-Blank Thing.   Keep a clean blackboard eraser in your car to use to wipe steam from your car windows. You can store it in the glove compartment, so it's handy when you need it.

Oh Wow! Look at the Snow!   Yeah, just look at it. Next, try getting it off the car without getting it all over yourself. Try using (keep this in the car) a plastic dustpan to scrape the snow off the car. It keeps you dry, and you won't mar the car's finish.

Where Are We?   You can keep the map you will be using extra handy by attaching it to the back of the sun visor with a clothespin. Saves the time you spend rummaging through the car trying to find the right map.

Garage It.   Take that extra minute or two to open the garage and park your car inside. A car parked inside the garage lasts longer than one subjected to the elements outside. And the garage makes life more difficult for car thieves.

And now I suppose you are going to tell me that there's no room for your car in the garage.

Sigh.

Fourteen

The Final Frontier

Being disorganized, it seems to me, is like gum disease. You mess around neglecting those gums for years. The dentist warns you. He gives you little horrifying meant-to-scare-the-pants-off-you pamphlets and screams at you to floss, floss, floss. You floss, sort of. Maybe once a week or so. You live with impending gum disease for years, really, until, one day it hits the bone, and now you can't function. Surgery is the only answer, and of course you have nobody to blame but yourself.

Disorganization is similar. You can live with it for years. You know it's not a great way to live, but you manage. Other people seem more concerned with your disorganization problem than you are. Then one day it dawns on you that you've got an organization problem of biblical proportions, and you need to get it fixed. Before it's too late. Now.

Nowhere is this more apparent than in the case of that wonderful attachment to the house known as the garage. For years we use it as our own personal dumping ground and way station for our things. You name it, it's probably out in the garage somewhere. D-Day finally dawns when you buy a new car and need a place to put it so the thieves can't get to it. Good luck. Chances are, you can't even get through the garage without a map—forget about getting an automobile in there. But wait a second. You *are* taking delivery on that car—this is no joke, you paid a fortune for that baby—and you are bound and determined to put it where it clearly belongs—in the garage.

You discuss the matter with your spouse. Come to think of it, says your wife, I think my mother's silver tea service is out there, and oh, honey, remember how wonderful you looked in your military uniform twenty years ago? And the letter sweater you got when you were a football star in college? Those things are out in the garage someplace—won't it be fun finding them?

Fun, indeed. Gum surgery is what it is, and like gum surgery, if you're smart you'll only do it once, and after that you'll behave yourself. Once the garage is organized you'll remember that the garage is *not* a storage unit, it is the home of your beautiful, incredibly expensive new car and perhaps some tools and stuff for the garden and grass. Therefore, the next time you find yourself moving something from the house to the garage, stop yourself before you get out the back door. Put the stuff where it *really* belongs right then and there . . . even if that place is the trash can. You'll save yourself some back-breaking time in the end. (Those of you who can swear to picture-perfect garages might want to sally forth to your attics or basements. While I'll be the first to admit that the *car* doesn't go in the attic or the basement, I'd also like to point out that neither does most of that other junk you've got crammed up or down there. The rules for keeping your garage organized—and the reasons for those rules—can also apply to that attic or basement.)

GO AT THE GARAGE

Once again you'll start by referring back to your "Getting Organized" goal. Turn to the project page that is titled "Organize the Garage" and check the steps required to get the job done. Do you need clean packing cartons? Will the roof need patching when you are finished? Do you want to let a charity know that they can make a pickup at the end of the day? Are you going to have a garage sale, and if so, can it be done the day after the clear out? By prioritizing the things to do and prepare for on your garage project page, you should be ready, willing, and positively able to march outside, fling open that garage door, and get started!

Start Early. Get up early and start early. I mean, as in eight o'clock, especially if it's a warm day. If it's autumn, you still need to start early, because you know perfectly well you'll want to stop and watch a little football (or run and do some shopping). An early start helps ensure that you actually get the whole job done while you have the mental and physical energy. First move everything out of the garage into an open area such as the backyard or driveway. Then sort everything with the following in mind:

Plan a Sale. Have a (you guessed it) *garage* sale. Get an early start, post lots of signs, and display your treasures and junk as attractively as possible. You'll sell everything from old underwear to furniture as long as you remember that people are looking for a *bargain*. If you want good (or even fair) prices, rent a storefront on Rodeo Drive or Madison Avenue.

Give It to Charity. Charities such as the Salvation Army, Goodwill, Saint Vincent de Paul, missions for the homeless, and shelters for battered women and abused children and runaways will be more than happy to receive your castoffs. Not only will you get a receipt good for a tax deduction, but you will have the satisfaction of knowing that you have helped others less fortunate than yourself.

Going, Going, Gone. If you have items of value such as antiques or collectibles that you are willing to part with, talk to an auctioneer about selling them for you. As long as you are willing to ask a low enough consignment price to allow a reasonable profit for the auctioneer and a good selling price to the buyer, the auctioneer will be able to sell the stuff for you.

Salvage Memories. Things that have some reason for being should be kept in their proper place, where they can be either used or adored. If you leave your high school yearbooks in the garage, they will only mildew and rot (although that might be a just fate, all things considered). If your yearbooks are meaningful to you, they should be in the house where they can be viewed and reminisced over periodically.

Bite the Bullet. Throw things away. That's right, trash them. Broken, rusty, bug-infested, mildewed, torn, or just plain useless items should be donated, without hesitation or remorse, to the trash bin.

Serve Notice. Call all the people who have been using your garage as a storage unit—and this includes the grown kids. Let them know that their lease is up and it's nonrenewable. Tell them you are renovating the garage (well, it will *look* renovated once it's cleaned out) and that they can store their belongings wherever they choose, as long as it's not in your house or garage. You have your own junk to contend with; you don't need theirs as well. Those away at college or off on a Tibetan retreat "finding themselves" can be notified that their belongings will be moved to a self-storage unit nearby. Don't forget to provide the address of the storage unit so that your beloved knows where to send the money to pay the bill.

Spider Watch. Here's what you should do if you come upon a male black widow spider. Kill him. Stomp him or whack him with the shovel. If you come across a female black widow spider, you should also stomp and whack the nasty little critter to death. The reason this saves you time, silly, is that if they bite you, you're off to the doctor's office, and we already know how much time and money that's going to take, especially since it's probably Saturday, the doctor is out playing golf, and you don't have an appointment.

Oh, Rats. A word here about little mousies. Mice are bad enough, but wait until you start dealing with rats in your garage. They can be tree rats or regular land rats—they love messed-up garages for some reason. There are lots of secret little places for them to hide and make their nests, where, as you can probably surmise, they multiply. My first experience with rats came when I took one of my workers to do a garage job in a very exclusive area. The client was moving, and she wanted to start packing and put the packed boxes in her garage. Trouble was, the garage was such a mess there was no room for anything. The car hadn't been in there for ages, and you could forget about adding more boxes. When we arrived she mumbled something about rats, but I brushed the matter off, thinking she was joking. She then went back into the house and only came out once in a while to check on our progress, jumping back with a screech every time we came upon more bugs and whatnot. The fact that she left the scene of the crime should have been my first clue. Most people are afraid I'll throw something precious away, so they stick around and watch like a hawk. Not only did she stay inside for the most part, she was willing to throw almost everything away or give it all to the Salvation Army. Just as I was thinking that this was the easiest garage we had ever done, we came across Ringo the Rat. Ringo, as I called him, was, thank God, quite dead. I noted (from a distance) that he apparently died in agony—his mouth was wide open, fangs bared in what appeared to be a last agonized gasp of some sort. The bugger was big—about fourteen inches long, I'd guess—and my worker swept him up and bagged him. Then, of course, we came across the nest. No other rats, baby or otherwise, were home, so we just swept it up. There was some dust. Cyanide dust, in fact.

We finished the job in record time, collected the money from the enormously grateful client, and chugged on back to the office. That night, I woke up gasping for air—probably like ol' Ringo had done in the end. This was followed by severe coughing attacks, rashes, and sinus problems. My worker, it turns out, had the same symptoms. We had been poisoned, probably by some cyanide dust or other residue when we swept up the nest and the dust around it. The client denied ever having any kind of exterminating process in her garage. This in spite of the fact she clearly knew about the rats and managed to stay out of the garage for most of the day. I didn't bother to point out to her that if, in fact, she did *not* have poison dusted in the garage, how was it that that monster Ringo died? Maybe he just checked out one day on his own. Like, rat suicide maybe.

The point is, before you clean out your garage, you might want to consider an extermination process for either the bugs or the rats. But if you do that, make sure you wait a good long time between the extermination and the clean out. Pesticide residue is very toxic for humans under certain circumstances, so don't take any chances. And then once you get the garage cleaned out, keep it that way, because bugs and rats are not nearly so fascinated by nice, clean, debris-free garages.

NOW USE THAT SPACE

Systemize. Hire someone (or do it yourself) to install shelves, sturdy hooks, and a drawer system (an old, beat-up dresser will suffice for the drawer system). Use these to hang and store auto parts, tools, gardening supplies, and the like.

Table It. If you do a lot of tinkering or gardening, give yourself a sturdy work table along one side of the garage—next to the window if you have one. You can use sawhorses and an old door. Having a table will help you keep the tools and supplies in one area instead of scattering things all over the yard, driveway, and into the house as you work.

Careful Storage. If you *must* store items other than auto and gardening supplies, be sure to pack the items carefully in clean, dry boxes, with easy-to-read, large labels on all sides of the box, and store the boxes, up off the floor, on a dry shelf.

Space Planning Made Simple. Now that you are heavily involved in the organize-the-garage/basement/attic-project, you just might want to give some consideration to exactly *how* you could creatively make use of this space that you have, complete with, at the very least, a roof and a floor of some kind. With some architectural changes, your basement or garage, and even your attic in some cases, could be turned into a rec room, a sewing or hobby room, an office, or a spare guest room. While this kind of "expansion" would involve a substantial money contribution on your part in most cases, it is not nearly as expensive as moving to a bigger house usually is. So once you've decided to clean the junk out of your storage space, think about how that area could just as easily be converted to happy living space.

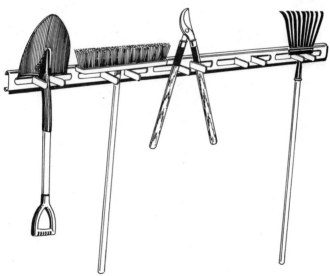

A simple rack such as this will help you keep the garage organized and give you more floor space at the same time.

Fifteen

Other People: Can They Be Helped?

Now that you've organized your time, some places, and lots of things, it's time to address the problem of the hordes of disorganized people surrounding you. They drive you nuts. You get organized, or were never that disorganized in the first place, but the troops around you are a mess. This might mean your kids, your spouse, your boss, or your employees are the problem. What, oh what, can you do to get them organized?

Probably not a whole heck of a lot.

The unfortunate truth is that you can't change someone who doesn't want to be changed. So, for the most part, you probably should get that notion (that you can make them get organized) out of your head. You can, however, make some progress on their disorganizational problem when it begins to affect your time and your life. There you can draw the line, put your foot down, whatever. How you do that can mean the difference between total failure and reasonable success, particularly if you are blessed/cursed with an assistant. How do you cure their bad, disorganizational, habits?

GOOD HELP IS HARD TO FIND

Assistants are great until you suddenly start to feel that you are in charge of two jobs—your own *and* the assistant's. You begin to feel you're always checking to make sure that your assistant is doing the job and doing it properly. Eventually you realize that you are in fact trapped, spending an inordinate amount of time with your assistant going over what needs to be done and how it should be done. Before you know it, you're making excuses to yourself about why you're not delegating tasks any more. "It's quicker if I do it myself. . . . It'll only get screwed up if he does it, and it won't be done on time. . . ." and so on. Soon you are so bogged down you can't think straight, and it's no wonder you never have any time for anything.

There is a solution to this problem. Not only will it help you ensure that others working with you are organized, but it will make the process of delegating workable, so that your time can be freed for some of the other projects that need your attention.

THE "PEOPLE" PAGE

Start by setting up another section in your notebook, titled "People." (If you have purchased a commercial planner, this section may already be on the divider.) Dayrunner, for instance, calls it "Persons." Whatever. They're "People" pure and simple, if you ask me.

Set up a page for each person that you deal with regularly (this might include, besides your assistant, the housekeeper, your boss, and if you are in business with your spouse or family, a page for them as well). Now, when you think of something to tell them, rather than dropping everything and either calling or going over to them to *interrupt* them (yes, you *do* interrupt people—you are not the only interruptee!), make a note on their particular page. Telling your thought or idea the minute you think of it, just so *you* won't forget, is not a good reason for you to interrupt them. A serious matter that absolutely cannot wait justifies an interruption, but otherwise simply make a note on your "People" page. Handling most discussion, delegation, and idea/information sharing via the "People" section makes life so much simpler that everybody naturally becomes more efficient in the process.

Once each day, preferably in the morning, sit down and have a ten-minute meeting with that person. Make sure this is an *uninterrupted* meeting—the other person deserves your full attention as much as you deserve his or hers. Briefly go over the items you have written on that person's page in your book, and note the date you discussed it next to each item. The following day, you will be able to see how projects that you previously delegated are coming along. This eliminates the worry that something isn't getting done, since the other person will come to understand that he or she will be held accountable on a daily basis (nicely, of course). By the same token, you might want to suggest to those other people that they do the same thing—set up a page for themselves with your name on it. That way, during your meeting, they can go over any questions or suggestions they might have had throughout the day.

When we talk about saving time, this simple method of communication and delegation by page has got to have the biggest reward. It saves tremendous amounts of time that are otherwise eaten up, bit by frustrating bit, through one of the most notorious time wasters of all—daily interruptions.

I once explained this "people" page concept to a thousand Tupperware distributors who had assembled from all parts of the country to share information and ideas. Tupperware distributors are generally husband-and-wife teams, so not only did they live together, they worked together as

PEOPLE

NAME _____

TODAYS DATE	DELEGATION · COMMUNICATION	DEADLINE	DONE

well. After my talk, one woman came up to me and said that although she had always made just such a list for her assistant, she had never thought to do it for the most important person of all—her husband! Instead, she would interrupt him constantly during the course of the day, simply so she wouldn't *forget*. She vowed to give her husband a page right then and there, and her husband, who was standing right next to her had, I must say, a rather large smile of relief on his face.

Set up your "People" section right behind your "Projects" section, and before your calendar. You'll want to do this because how you interact with those people on a daily basis, and what you delegate to them, will, in large part, contribute to how you then schedule your own time. Remember to pencil in the date you delegated or passed along the project information, and while you're at it, write in a deadline for each project, so that there's no confusion later on that always ends up with excuses like, "But I didn't know. . . . You didn't tell me that. . . ." and so forth. (Conversely, if you are the assistant and your boss keeps saying she told you something when you know darned well she did not, this system should catch up the boss as well. It really works at clarifying communication for everybody.) With your "People" page you have an automatic daily communication, delegation, status report that defies most of the common excuses you are likely to otherwise hear.

BOSS-ASSISTANT EFFECTIVENESS

Along with your "People" page, here are some additional tips that will help eliminate some of that extra work and thus free you to become more productive at the same time. Also, it will probably improve the working relationship between you and your assistant, and boosting morale can only be helpful.

Prioritize. Be clear about which projects have the highest priority. You did this for yourself earlier in the book; now you need to include that system of prioritizing when you give directions to those who work for or with you. This is particularly important if an emergency throws the normal work routine off schedule. Be certain to tell your assistant, as he or she reschedules everything, what takes priority, not only for the emergency at hand, but also after everyone gets back to the daily work at hand. Remember, this is *not* a circus you're all taking part in.

Clarify the Chain of Command. If other people use your assistant—and the word *use* is certainly appropriate here—make certain that everyone understands the chain of command and the priorities within that chain. Nothing is more frustrating to an assistant than to have three people assigning projects, each insisting that his or hers is *absolutely* the most critical matter of the day.

Communicate. Assistants are not mind-readers. Let your assistant know what results you expect on any given project, or to put it another way, the goals you expect to reach. A detailed explanation with periodic updates to answer and clarify questions can make all the difference in your assistant's work performance.

Set Deadlines. Again, you set deadlines for yourself, and you need to include them in your instructions to those who work for you. Establish time lines, in writing if necessary, and then make certain your assistant responds to them with finished projects. Not knowing exactly when something needs to be done often causes assistants to juggle their workload in a manner that would probably horrify you at the very least.

Appreciate. Be liberal with compliments for jobs well done, no matter how small. Saying thank you often will help give you the freedom to point out poor performance in a constructive, nonthreatening manner. Remember, too, when you offer up a criticism, that it should be of the *work done*, that is, the behavior, or poor work turned in, and not a criticism of the *person*. People respond to criticism much better if they understand that you are not criticizing them personally, and if they know that you appreciate their good work performance as well.

Follow the Paper-Sorting Principles. Insist that your assistant follow the paper-sorting principles outlined in the Papernoia chapter. This means that both of you will be handling matters consistently, which then means that you will operate more effectively as a team as well as independently. The paper sorting includes the categories To Do, To Pay, To File, and To Read (and of course that all important To Toss!). It also especially includes the fact that your assistant never be allowed to put work in progress in his or her desk drawers. This dangerous habit, as you know, leads to lost paperwork and forgotten and therefore uncompleted tasks. Drawers are for supplies and personal effects only. A few ratty tea bags are fine. The half-finished report to the board of directors is not.

Have a Sensible Out Basket. Take the time to write clear instructions on the work that your assistant takes from your "out" basket. Write legibly and clearly, and you'll avoid a lot of unnecessary interruptions that occur because questions constantly crop up.

Know Your Assistant's Job and How to Do It if You Have To. It's tempting to give work to an assistant, supposedly secure in the knowledge that it will all be "taken care of, somehow." The fact is, you lose a significant amount of control over your department, work flow, and the assistant when you don't know exactly what it is that gets done at that position, much less how it's actually done. You don't have to *do* the work, you just have to know how it actually gets done. Your rewards are the freedom to fire that person when necessary and the independence to function temporarily in his or her absence. Let's face it, assistants, from time to time, disappear. They get married, leave town, and get run over by trucks. Make like the Scouts and be prepared. You'll be ever so much better off.

Tidy Up. How many times do we have to put this one in here? We had it in the kitchen and for your desk and paperwork, and we even alluded to it ever so briefly in the housework section (after all, if housework doesn't sometimes translate into "tidy up," I don't know what does), and now here it is again. Ask your assistant to spend the final fifteen minutes of the day organizing the work on the top of his or her work station (desk, credenza, whatever). It will be easier for you to find something if you need to (and the assistant isn't in), and the assistant won't feel so overworked and hassled when the next day is started—like yours of course—with a neat desk.

Set an Example. Treat your assistant as you would like to be treated—in a fair, businesslike manner—and you will be amazed at the increased quality in your assistant's attitude toward you as well as toward the work at hand. This is also known as "Do unto others as you would have them do unto you."

If you *are* the assistant or secretary, what do you do? After all, you can't fire the boss or even make the boss get organized. What you can do is take the tips for the boss working with the assistant, and turn them around so they work for you:

- *ASK THE BOSS WHAT THE PRIORITIES ARE.*

- *ASK WHAT RESULTS ARE EXPECTED ON ANY GIVEN PROJECT.*

- *ASK IF THERE ARE DEADLINES, AND IF SO, WHAT THEY ARE.*

- *ASK TO HAVE THE CHAIN OF COMMAND CLARIFIED, ESPECIALLY IF EVERYBODY IS DUMPING STUFF ON YOU.*

- *FOLLOW THE PAPER-SORTING PRINCIPLE, AND TRY TO GET THE BOSS TO DO THE SAME.*

- *ASK THE BOSS TO WRITE CLEAR INSTRUCTIONS ON THE WORK IN THE OUT BASKET.*

- *COMMUNICATE DAILY BY HAVING A "PEOPLE"*

PAGE OF YOUR OWN FOR THE BOSS (this way, the boss knows you know exactly what was or wasn't said, assigned, or delegated).

- *TREAT YOUR BOSS WITH RESPECT, AND AT THE SAME TIME LET THE BOSS KNOW THAT YOU EXPECT NO LESS IN RETURN.*

- *COMPLIMENT A JOB WELL DONE. JUST BECAUSE SOMEONE IS YOUR BOSS DOESN'T MEAN THAT HE OR SHE DOESN'T APPRECIATE APPRECIATION.*

That should help you with your organizational efforts at work. But what about more dangerous ground—at home, for instance? Take the recalcitrant, and most probably surly, teenager, for starters.

CAN YOU ORGANIZE A TEENAGER?

If you've got teenagers, chances are, you know the real meaning of the word *chaos.* If they were out of control in the mess department when they were little, now they are probably ready to enter the twilight zone of the totally, hopelessly disorganized. Add to this their general attitude—not always the greatest—and you can have a real problem on your hands. You could always shut the door to their room and forget about it, but we all know full well that if they don't learn how to get organized now, they'll grow up to be slobs, and we also know who will get the ultimate blame for that character defect—you, the loving parent, that's who.

To help fend off that potential bad rap, here's some advice on getting that obstinate little rascal organized before it's too late.

Teen Project. As with everything else, this could be outlined on a project page in your planner notebook. But more than that, see if you can get the teen to set up a similar book geared to her specific needs—and of course insist on a "Get Organized" project with the appropriate priority level. Teens may want to stall and put their other projects (the more fun ones, of course) up front, but this is where a good, firm *no* can come in handy. Remember to explain the expected results/benefits to the teen in a way that it will seem to benefit him as well as you. I've taught young adolescents the Five-Step Life Management Plan and have had their mothers call me to say that they were discussing their "six-month goals" over dinner. If you'll think about it, how much grief and learning time would have been spared had you been taught sensible time and organizational-management skills early in life?

Easy Does It. Working with the Project page outline, decide on a time frame and inform your teen of the deadline and your expectations. Tell your child that he or she is going to get organized, and you (or someone) is going to help. It is imperative that you remain calm. The teen may try to get hysterical. Ignore that tactic; it is meant to wear you down.

Joint Effort. Let the teen know that he or she will be participating on every level. Many of the decisions will, furthermore, fall to the teen, and some of those will actually be fun and challenging. The project should not be perceived, or in any way presented, as "work." Rather it is a "project," and should be viewed to some extent as a challenge and a goal that will bring its own rewards once achieved.

Activities/Opportunities Management. Remind not only yourself but your teen that by completing this project, one and all will be blessed with more time to enjoy the activities and opportunities that come their way. You'll save time in the nagging and picking-up-after departments, and the teen will save the time it takes to think of ways to get out of cleaning up the mess daily, not to mention the time that was previously wasted trying to find things that needed to be found.

Needy. Understand the teen's needs. More than that, allow the teen to decide what he or she needs. If he wants to display his model car collection, let him. Just make sure it's displayed on sturdy, useful bookshelves that can later be used for books. Whatever a teen needs today is probably not what he or she will need eight months from now. So let them outline their needs, but accommodate them in a manner that will allow for future fads, wants, and needs.

Call for Help. If your teen is hostile, consider hiring an outside organizer to help with the project. They can come in and do the job with an objectivity that may be difficult for you to muster up. Invariably, with parent and child, it becomes a "you do it or else" situation, which is almost always counterproductive, and while it might get the job done, out of spite if nothing else, the teen probably won't keep the room organized once it's finished.

Decorate. Be prepared to do a little decorating. Some new items for the room, whether a new desk or a new cover for the bed, can add incentive, and in most cases, the room will need some updating anyway.

Baskets, Bins, and Doodads. Baskets, bins, and industrial-type containers are very popular right now, and are versatile enough to adapt to the teen's changing needs. And if the teen by chance gets sick of them, these containers can be moved and used in another part of the house. An example of this is a blueprint bin. Made originally for blueprints, this wonderful item will accommodate fishing poles, skis, golf clubs, and any number of unwieldy items. It's on casters and therefore easily moved. You could even use it later to store brooms and mops in the utility closet.

Shelve It. There is nothing quite as accommodating as shelving. You can do it yourself and paint the shelves to match the decor. Once up, shelving handles collections, trophies, albums, etc., until the teen leaves home. Then (it will happen, *someday*) you can always dismantle it and use it somewhere else, even if it's only in the garage.

Cure the Closet. Take this opportunity to have a good closet system installed. The systems on the market today can easily double and triple the closet space you currently have. If you can do it in your room, you can do it in theirs. Your property value will be further enhanced, and a good system will take your student right through college and still be suitable for the room, regardless of its eventual use or occupant.

Gee, Mom, This Is Awesome. Emphasize pride. This is a project that can be a source of pleasure and pride for everyone concerned. I once did a teen's room, and the minute it was done, all of his friends "happened" by to take a tour. I'm convinced that he will keep his room looking "awesome," as he called it, and that he will remember the process of getting organized well enough to avoid turning into the dreaded grown-up slob.

There are a few ideas on the almighty teen. Good luck, and God bless.

YOURS, MINE, AND OURS

And, moving bravely along, what about spouses? Or live-ins, or lovers, or boyfriends and girlfriends? Mates? The other half? Them? What can you do to make them shape up?

You could see a therapist and spend lots of money trying to figure out why you, a perfectly organized person, picked this person, who is a disorganized slob, to love. You could do that.

Or, you could nag yourself into a divorce and/or a nervous breakdown. You could do that.

Or, you can live by the Yours, Mine, and Ours creed. That's the ever-lovin' philosophy that says that, contrary to traditional beliefs, it is not really all *ours*. There's *yours*. There's *mine*. And there's *ours*. And, if you're smart you'll set it up that way, and keep it that way. There are no quick tips to save you on this one. Just the Yours, Mine, and Ours to keep you out of the therapist's office and the divorce courts.

Basically, the idea goes like this. They want to make and live in a mess, fine. That's their mess. They can have it. Map out an area—a room, the garage, the dining alcove—and call it theirs. If you can shut the door on it, all the better. If you can't—say it's a corner in a too-small apartment—learn to wear blinders when you pass by that area. Remember, it's theirs. Then, there's yours. Pristine. Perfectly perfect. Yours. As in, keep your cotton pickin' disorganized paws off of, and out of, this part of the house. It's mine. Then there's ours. This is where you actually commingle and compromise. Your other person will have to tidy up a bit. You'll have to loosen up your standards a bit. Compromise in the name of the relationship. You don't have to sacrifice all your organized ethics, but you'll probably have to let go of some of them. And the *they* in your life will have to incorporate a little shaping up into their (dis)orderly routine. Thus you come to that all-loving state known as *ours*.

Sooner or later every relationship, in my opinion, hits a crisis point over how things are kept up around the place. I believe that those couples who opt for the Yours, Mine, and Ours method of environmental matrimony pass through the crisis with not only more wisdom and love in their hearts, but a sense that each part of the couple has actually *won* the battle to have it their way. Since each of you thinks you have won, each of you will head into the next twenty years with a satisfied, albeit smug, little smirk on your face and in your heart.

And I'd be the last person on earth to destroy that illusion, and if you want your relationship to survive a simple thing like disorganization, you'll adjust to, and come to love, the Yours, Mine, and Ours system of doing things and loving each other.

Sixteen

Now That You're Finally Organized

Congratulations. You've finished what you started—this book! No doubt you've done a little organizing along the way, and once you close the book, you'll go on to do more. And it can't have been easy, I know that. But it was really *for your own good*.

And now that you're finally organized, or at the very least, well on your way to being organized, you may be just a bit worried about how you are going to manage to *stay* organized. Some of the tips that worked to *get* you organized are the same tips that you can use in order to *stay* organized:

1. MAKE PLANS AND GOALS, AND USE DEADLINES TO ACHIEVE THOSE PLANS AND GOALS AS THEY RELATE TO YOUR MISSION IN LIFE.

2. USE A LIST SYSTEM.

3. REMEMBER TO PRIORITIZE.

4. STICK TO YOUR SCHEDULE (BUT REMEMBER FLEXIBILITY).

5. REMEMBER TO SAY NO.

6. CONSOLIDATE OR GROUP ERRANDS AND TASKS.

7. DELEGATE.

8. MAKE CONSTRUCTIVE USE OF YOUR WAITING TIME.

9. CLEAN UP AS YOU GO.

10. PUT THINGS AWAY WHEN YOU ARE FINISHED WITH THEM.

11. OPEN AND SORT YOUR MAIL THE MINUTE YOU RECEIVE IT.

12. DON'T BUY ANYTHING UNLESS YOU HAVE A PLACE TO PUT IT.

13. DON'T BUY THINGS JUST BECAUSE THEY ARE ON SALE.

14. REFUSE TO BUY THINGS THAT NEED SPECIAL ATTENTION AND CARE.

15. REWARD YOURSELF REGULARLY FOR YOUR ORGANIZATIONAL SKILLS.

And, last, but not least, now that you are finally organized, you can do projects by breaking them down into segments. Projects or tasks that seem overwhelming to you can be accomplished if you attack the entire project in more tolerable sections. For example, if you have an important report to write, rather than telling yourself that you have to take two entire days to do nothing but that report, break it down. Spend two hours assembling the research. Do other chores or tasks.

Come back to the report and spend thirty minutes to put the facts in chronological order. The following day start by spending two hours checking the facts, and possibly, making some calls regarding the report. And so on. Before you know it, the report is done. And, instead of cramming it into two nerve-racking days at the last possible minute, if you start on it when you get the assignment, and do it in more tolerable time segments, chances are you will finish not only on time but possibly even ahead of time. Plus, it's a good bet that the report will be written in a more concise, organized manner, which means that whoever reads it will be that much more appreciative of your expertise and talents, and making those kinds of good impressions on other people can only help you in the long run.

By breaking down a task into manageable time segments, whether it's a report or the laundry (if you do two weeks' laundry all at once, it will take forever, and you'll hate it—in fact, probably the only reason you finally do the dreaded deed is because you are completely out of clean underwear) you will trick yourself into thinking that the chore is not really so bad after all. And you know what? It really isn't so bad—when you're organized. Remember, it's not where you start, it's where you finish that counts!

Speaking of finished, now that you've come to the end of this book, one of your rewards is that I've got a confession to make that you will no doubt enjoy rather more than you should. And that is that I am not really so organized myself. Maybe I mess up because I don't have enough, er, time.

Whatever it is, I know that I used to be perfectly, compulsively organized. I still have one friend who remembers, years ago, staying at my apartment as a houseguest. He slept on my sofa bed in the living room and awoke each morning without fail (Sundays included) to the roar of the vacuum cleaner. I had a brown carpet and couldn't tolerate even the tiniest bit of lint on it. So I jumped up out of bed each and every day and first thing, *vacuumed*. That should give you an idea of the extreme measures I went to to get organized. This does not mean that I cleaned the bathtub every day, however.

Cleaning is not the same as vacuuming, somehow—don't ask me why.

Anyway, I went on like this for years—all through my twenties—and one day, wouldn't you know it, I hit thirty. I scraped up enough money to slap a down payment on a car (I hadn't driven in twelve years), put my last $250 in my pocket, and headed from New York to California. I cried all the way to Pennsylvania, but by the next day I was in Ohio, and bingo, suddenly I could see it all. California, here I come!

That move changed my life. In California they don't vacuum every day. Everybody is too "laid back." Still, I did it for about the first three years or so until I finally added up all the time that daily vacuuming took and decided that maybe I should join everybody else and jump into some shorts and head for the beach instead.

Then there was the matter of all my *stuff*. Do you know what movers would like to charge you to move things from New York to California? Forget it. Your destination might just as well be Mars. Rockefeller would probably turn pale. Because of the cost, I ended up selling nearly everything and giving away the rest. I took a terrible loss and learned a valuable lesson: Not only does it cost you in time to keep all this stuff straightened up and cleaned, it costs you to move it like you can't believe. So I started over with nothing and came to understand that *less is more*. Because in five years, somehow, I accumulated another houseful of stuff, and I looked around and found myself vacuuming every day again. So I pitched more things, and now if I buy, I don't buy what I don't need, and I don't get anything unless I have a place to put it.

By the time I hit 35, I was getting pretty relaxed about a lot of things. Then I went into business as an organizer, and guess what? At first I worked out of my house, and really, there wasn't room in that place for everything. The desk was in a corner by the kitchen, and I had boxes of stuff all over the place. And it really didn't bother me too much, because I'd gone from being a compulsive about how I spent my personal time (overorganizing) to someone who was a little bit on the Missy Messy side.

Periodically I'd get rid of things—have a garage sale, clean out the files, whatever. But the boxes were still by the recliner, and projects stacked here and there. I couldn't let a client near the place. It wasn't bad, you understand, just not terribly good. This all came to a head when I took an extended business trip and returned to find that my place had been "organized" by a friend in my absence. He had painted and papered some walls (very nice) and somehow managed to eliminate all the clutter. I thought it was great until I started to do what all my clients tend to do—panic. Where's my . . . and where's my . . .? "Look," he said impatiently, "I didn't throw anything away, so relax!" I did locate everything, since he was telling the truth—he really hadn't tossed everything. But one day I was foraging in the hall closet and happened to try to move the airline-size cat carrier. It wouldn't budge. I opened it up and found about twenty books, stashed there by my overzealous friend in an effort to clear the overburdened bookcases. Pointing out that should there be a natural disaster, like an earthquake, the cats were to be shunted into the carrier didn't faze my organizing friend. He could only see that there were too many books on the bookcases, and in my neatnik New York days, I would have agreed. Now it really didn't matter to me that much, but after he organized me I vowed to keep the book clutter down by telling myself that when the bookcase gets full, some books get given away. It's a self-monitoring system that keeps everybody relatively happy.

And now? Now, I'm thirty-nine, and I'm not a perfectionist and I'm not a slob. I'm somewhere in between, and I think it's going to work out all right. I'm thinking that next year I'm going to move, but this time the movers won't be able to terrify me like they did before. Because now I've got an office, which is neat, and I've got where I live, which is neat enough. And instead of spending my time being compulsively organized, I've settled for functional and comfortable. And most of all, I've settled for the extra time in my life that attitude brings me—time to make the most of the life that I have.

And now that you're organized, who knows? If you'll give up that daily quest for perfection (like I did with the vacuuming) and settle for functional, productive, and comfortable, like I have, maybe you'll have the time to do as I have done: hang out a shingle and go into business for yourself as a professional organizer. Remember, if you decide to do that, though, your time will have to be analyzed and spent very carefully in order to grow in your business and help those disorganized people who come to you to reach that state of perfection that they think they need. Consider this very special letter that I received from a man who read about me in a local magazine:

> Dear Stephanie Culp:
>
> This letter would not be written had I not chanced, yesterday, in a lawyer's waiting room, to open a somewhat whiskered copy of a magazine to the right page and glimpse the word, *organizer.*
>
> A *professional* organizer! Bells rang. And as I read, caught up in your story, the photo on the page might have changed to that of another woman—one not so youthful, but no less dedicated to Edna St. Vincent Millay's proposition that "order is a lovely thing." And I thought you might like to know about the parallel.
>
> Lyla—tireless and resolute in the business of what Webster calls "systematic relationships," or, "grouping according to kind or sequence of use." Had she known that it paid money, she'd have joined the Union. But she did recognize organization as an art—one profitably studied in the supermarkets where, right beside the strawberries, is the shortcake.
>
> Lyla's talent developed early; first by housekeeping at 12; then by years on the road where she learned in packing theatre trunks, how to get a quart of stuff into a pint bottle.
>
> You'd have to see it to believe it. Or better yet, live with it; open a drawer or cabinet and it would be packed solid, complete with an inventory card system! Hundreds of spools of thread, graded like a color chart. Fifty-two pairs of shoes in plastic boxes. An effi-

ciency diagram for every errand trip by car, with appropriate phone calls beforehand. Every container of leftovers in the fridge had a date. Every one of a thousand boxes had a label; "Batik from Bali," "Old Garters and Girdles," "My Baby Clothes."

You see, Lyla was one of your Savers. Thrifty? Asked if she had ever read the *Mormon Book of Thrift*, she snorted, "Read it? I *wrote* it!"

She never missed a trick. She had a map of all the thrift stores in the county and ran a trapping line to each one of them. She had a file box of coupons. Stacked in the garage were four forty-pound cartons of homemade soap. Every spring she hand-washed all of her drapes and ironed them, and after twenty-four years, they still looked near new. Strawberry runners went into the veg-tray of the fridge for a twenty-day dormancy period before replanting. And when the front door chimes wouldn't bong twice, as required to distinguish them from the back, she printed in the nameplate space, "PLEASE PUSH TWICE."

The living room held enough for the Smithsonian; crystals in a sunlit obelisk scattered shards of rainbow everywhere. Three big curio cabinets that she had made herself were filled with incunabula gathered in a trip to the Orient. She'd saved a foot warmer, complete with carpet cover and bricks, from her childhood buggy days in rural Nebraska. An exquisite silk wall screen, Chinese, covered most of one wall. All and everything was included in her photographic inventories.

What possessed her? Maybe you can tell.

Widowed in 1953, she went to work at a shop in Pasadena where she worked on straight commission. She kept her own records on her customers—sizes, color preferences, even social engagements that she had gleaned from the society columns so that she could phone the customer when the right coat or dress came in. She taught Sunday school for twenty-two years, and it took a U-Haul to send back to the church all of the visual aids and records she kept on her students. She had friends in every profession and loved them all. She never missed a birthday or an anniversary. She was organized. And somehow, she accumulated a fortune from being that way.

Lyla never objected to my shucking my clothes in a heap on the floor, but did have other concerns: "I pity the poor man who has to clean out this house," she said, looking straight at me. "But just don't *give* everything away—*sell* the stuff!" This was after the doctor gave her the bad news about her lungs.

She rests now under the quiet winds of Rose Hills, unaware that her possessions were, after all, given away to friends. I don't tell her. But I'm going to mention that she could make money as a professional organizer.

That should bring her back!

Hope I haven't bored you!

Sincerely,

And the letter was signed with the name of a man who has made me promise not to reveal his name, and so I won't.

But when I speak in front of groups now, I often close my talk with the story of Lyla. And, like her husband who wrote me that letter, I hope I haven't bored you.

Appendix A

APPOINTMENT/PLANNER SYSTEMS

WEEK-AT-A-GLANCE
Available at most stationery stores

PLUS This oldie but goodie is produced by Sheaffer Eaton, and is available at nearly all stationery stores. This is only a calendar planner, but it is one of the best there is available. This is the perfect addition to your own three-ring binder if you decide not to buy one of the other fancy planners. If you are looking for something inexpensive, this is the way to go, and it'll get the job done.

MINUS None except the obvious — it's not a total system and doesn't even come close to being one.

PRICE Unbeatable at under $10.00

DAYRUNNER
Available at better department stores and office supply stores.

PLUS The very popular Dayrunner and Runningmate planners come in a wide range of attractive binders with styles to accommodate nearly everyone. Some of the graphics on their inserts are top-notch. I especially like their index tabs because of their bright clarity, and their movable page marker is a wonderful device that lets you turn automatically to the desired section in your book. Dayrunner continues to stay ahead of the market in design innovation, which means that it's always worth your time to stop at the Dayrunner display to see what's new.

MINUS Some of their inserts, such as Goals and Projects, are, in my opinion, too fussy and overcomplicated. Also, when you buy the book, you get only a sampling of inserts; you will find yourself running back to the store many times over the course of the year to buy more. Also, Harper House, as of this writing, does not include instructions on how best to use their book — a serious oversight as far as I'm concerned.

PRICE Dayrunner systems range from moderately priced to expensive.

DAY-TIMERS, INC.
(Send for catalog)
IN USA
DAY-TIMERS, INC.
Allentown, PA 18001
215/395-5884

Also available by mail in Canada, the United Kingdom, Australia, and New Zealand.

PLUS This is, in my opinion, the best system on the market. It really is a "design-it-yourself" system since it is easily converted to suit the individual user's particular needs. Setting up the Five Step Plan (plus the People section) in this book is a snap. You'll want to order the "Activity Binder" and the appropriate insert pages for it. Their pages are wonderfully simple, yet concise, and they offer a selection that accommodates just about every possible situation. And for people who don't want to carry a book around, their Pocket Day-Timer is an ingenious wallet-sized system that serves as a calendar and mini-planner that works well either along with the Activity Binder, or as a simple mini time organizer in itself.

MINUS I can't think of anything about this system that would be considered a drawback unless you think ordering by mail is a drawback. I think ordering by mail is great—it saves time!

PRICE The price range here goes from inexpensive to expensive, depending on the system you select.

FILOFAX
Available at select department stores, design stores, men's and women's specialty stores, stationery stores, luggage and leather stores, and museums, including the Museum of Modern Art in New York. For more information write:
The Londonhouse Corp.
(Exclusive Agent and Licensee)
3330 Ocean Park Blvd.
Santa Monica, Calif 90405-3284

PLUS This is, without question, the most beautiful system on the market. It only sells in leather, and the insert pages are so lovely that one almost hates to write on them. If you're looking for looks, this is the only book to buy.

MINUS Unfortunately, with all its beauty, Filofax is a little short on the practicality end. You will definitely be buying insert pages throughout the year, and it will cost you more than plenty. Setting up your beginning system can be confusing, because while Filofax offers a fabulous array of insert pages with amazing things on them, many times the shop will be out of the most practical inserts, such as index tabs or the new calendar. Also, the book comes in one size only, so if you aren't a small writer, this isn't for you.

PRICE Don't even look at this system unless money is no object.

Appendix B

CAR SAFETY

Please Call Police Signs

In the chapter "Car Crazy" I discussed the possibility of assault when a woman motorist is stranded with a disabled automobile. Along with the possibility of assault, motorists with disabled vehicles run into traffic. The California Highway Patrol says that in California alone there are 20,000 accidents involving people who have exited from their disabled vehicle and been hit by another vehicle, or in some way created another accident situation. Also, the Westside Center for Independent Living points out that people with disabilities are often physically unable to get out of their vehicle, and because of this, the Please Call Police sign is an invaluable aid to them when their vehicle breaks down. Elderly people might find the sign especially beneficial. In fact, I think it's a great idea for just about everybody's personal safety. The signs can be ordered through the nonprofit organization (listed below). Your donation is tax deductible, and any profit realized by your purchase goes to further aid those organizations in their work.

WESTSIDE CENTER FOR INDEPENDENT LIVING
P.O. Box 66980
Los Angeles, CA 90066

Send WCIL $5 per sign. The center provides training and support services to people with disabilities.

KITCHEN

Tupperware

Check your telephone white pages under "Tupperware Home Parties." If no distributorship listing appears in your directory, write to:

TUPPERWARE HOME PARTIES
Consumer Relations Department
P.O. Box 2353
Orlando, FL 32802

PLUS In business since 1951, Tupperware is becoming something of an American tradition. Just about everyone has some Tupperware kicking around in their kitchen, and that may be because Tupperware offers a lifetime guarantee on their products against chipping, cracking, breaking, or peeling (under normal use). Many people swear nothing keeps food fresh as well as Tupperware does. Besides their reliable food storage containers, they've added some nifty space-saving items, including their Modular Mates Rack (this will increase cupboard space), Modular Mates Refrigerator Rack (great for increasing your refrigerator space), Modular Keeper (another nifty refrigerator item), Modular Carousel (this one has a million possible uses, and can also clip to a refrigerator shelf to hang down and save space) and Seal Organizers (these neatly hold the tops to the food storage containers—Tupperware calls them seals because they "seal" in the freshness of the food). They've also got a Dining Tray that is great for making and freezing meals in advance. Finally, one of the best, and, as far as I know, unique, services available from a Tupperware dealer is their "Custom Kitchen Planning" consultation. The Tupperware dealer will come to your home and show you how to store more food, particularly staples, in less space (by using their products, of course). This really works, and for the money, you can't beat this offer of one-on-one organizational advice.

MINUS You do have to order through a dealer—there's no hopping down to the local mart for a piece of Tupperware. On the other hand, you can't beat having, as Tupperware says, "personal service and friendly professionalism from a qualified food storage consultant."

PRICE Each piece is moderately priced, and all quite affordable (particularly when you consider their lifetime guarantee).

ORGANIZING RACKS AND SYSTEMS

Closet Maid

Closet Maid products are sold nationally in hardware and department stores, home centers and specialty stores. For the name and address of your nearest supplier, call the manufacturer toll free:

CLAIRSON INTERNATIONAL
20 South West 17th Street
Ocala, FL 32674
Telephone (in Florida) 1-800-421-0104
(nationally) 1-800-221-0641

PLUS For organization, you really can't beat Closet Maid's rolling basket systems. They can be used for any number of things, can be stored in closets or the garage, and look just fine out in the open in some areas of the home or office. I love these things; I've got 'em, and all of my clients have them too. Closet Maid also makes ventilated organizer kits, shelving, racks, and other storage accessories that are available either as installed storage systems (out here in California, for example, the Closet Store in Los Angeles designs and installs the Closet Maid system to fit your closet), or you can buy do-it-yourself kits and components. There are a lot of ways to use Closet Maid, not only in closets but in laundry areas, the garage, the kitchen, and the kids' rooms. It's versatile organization that really does a good job.

MINUS I love the baskets to death, and their closet systems do a nifty job too, but do remember that these are wire shelving units, which means that you can't put itty-bitty things on the shelf unless you lay down a sheet of Plexiglas or something first—otherwise the itty-bitty stuff will fall through the wires. Except for that, Closet Maid is a real winner.

PRICE Moderate to expensive, depending on the extent of the system you choose to buy.

Rubbermaid

Available at discount variety stores, supermarkets, and drugstores, or contact (for order information):

RUBBERMAID
Consumer Service Department
1147 Akron Road
Wooster, OH 44691

PLUS Rubbermaid is everywhere, with a wide range of products that includes everything from laundry baskets to turntables. I'm especially impressed with Rubbermaid's concentrated effort to "conquer space" with their line of space-saving organizers. These are their "storage products," and they include some fabulous install-it-yourself goodies. Look for their Wall-Mounted Shelf & Drawer (great for the children's room, laundry room, garage, or closets), their Pull-Out Tray (try this under the sink or in a bathroom cabinet), their Wrap & Bag Organizer (goodbye to bags between the refrigerator and the wall, and hello to some order with the plastic wrap), their Ironing Organizer (allows you to hang the iron on the wall with the iron and spray starch above it), the Clean-Up Organizer (another good one for under the sink to hold cleaning supplies), their Mop & Broom Organizer (lets you hang mop, broom, and dustpan on wall or inside closet), their Under Shelf Bin (gives you a bit more shelf space), and of course, their Instant Drawer Organizers (these come in a multitude of sizes to fit any drawer) and their fabulous Turntables, which help organize any number of things in the bathroom or the kitchen cabinets.

MINUS It's almost impossible to find fault with Rubbermaid; once again I see to it that my clients use Rubbermaid, because I use it myself. The only item in their extensive line of products that I have a bit of a problem with is their Stackable Storage Bins that tend to get cumbersome to use when full. Except for that, Rubbermaid gets my wholehearted organizational vote.

PRICE Inexpensive to moderate.

MAIL-ORDER ORGANIZATION

Hold Everything
This delightful mail-order catalogue by Williams-Sonoma is devoted to organizational products. To receive the current catalogue, write:
WILLIAMS-SONOMA
Mail Order Department
P.O. Box 7456
San Francisco, CA 94120-7456
PLUS Mail order is always a plus; you save time by ordering from your armchair, and with this catalogue you can save time and get the supplies you need to get organized at the same time. The catalogue offers all types of products from closet organizers to kitchen and office organizers.

MINUS There is no minus to this catalogue; they do offer a wide range of products. Watch yourself, though. Don't order a container or item just because it is pretty or sleek looking. Make sure that you have a useful purpose for it once it gets to you.

PRICE The catalogue is free. The items in the catalogue range in price from inexpensive to moderate.

Index

Other Books of Interest

Slow Down . . . and Get More Done, by Marshall Cook. Find the right pace for your life by gaining control of worry, making possibilities instead of plans, and putting diet and exercise in perspective. 192 pages, $11.95, paperback

Confessions of a Happily Organized Family, by Deniece Schofield. Learn how to work together as a family to restore (or establish) a comfortable sense of order to your home. You'll find specific techniques for making mornings less hectic, traveling with kids, making chores fun, and more. 246 pages, $10.95, paperback

Organized Closets & Storage: Ideas for Every Room In Your Home, by Stephanie Culp. Culp takes a walking tour of your home, looking at storage areas room by room and offering alternative solutions to existing problems. Dozens of full-color photographs, tips from organizational experts, and a directory listing of products shown make this the comprehensive guide to closet and storage problems. 128 pages, 80 color illus., $3.99, paperback

Conquering The Paper Pile-Up, by Stephanie Culp. If you're inundated with paper — mail, school papers, insurance forms, bills, correspondence, business records — and who isn't, this is the book for you. Culp cures your "papernoia" with tips on how to sort, organize, file, and store every piece of paper in your home or office. 176 pages, $11.95, paperback

How To Conquer Clutter, by Stephanie Culp. Think of this book as a "first aid guide" for when you wake up and find that clutter has once again overtaken every inch of available space you have. This book offers A-to-Z help for clutter-bound souls who long for a clutter-free life. 160 pages, $10.95, paperback

It's Here . . . Somewhere!, by Alice Fulton & Pauline Hatch. Fulton and Hatch show you how to get more places out of your spaces with their *room-by-room* approach to getting your home in order. 179 pages, $10.95, paperback

Use this coupon to order your copies today!

YES! Please send me:
_____ (70183) Slow Down . . . and Get More Done, $11.95
_____ (1145) Confessions of a Happily Organized Family, $10.95
_____ (10119) How to Conquer Clutter, $10.95
_____ (10214) It's Here . . . Somewhere!, $10.95
_____ (10161K) Organized Closets & Storage, $3.99
_____ (10178) Conquering The Paper Pile-Up, $11.95
(Please add $3.00 postage & handling for one book, $1.00 for each additional book. Ohio residents add 5½% sales tax.)

☐ Payment enclosed
☐ Please charge my: ☐ Visa ☐ MasterCard (Minimum charge order: $10)

Acct. # _____/_____/_____/_____ Exp. Date _____

Signature _____

Name _____

Address _____

City _____ State _____ Zip _____

Send to: Writer's Digest Books,   Credit card orders call
          1507 Dana Avenue,   TOLL-FREE 1-800-289-0963
          Cincinnati, Ohio 45207

(PRICES SUBJECT TO CHANGE WITHOUT NOTICE)

6391

About the Author

Organization and time management expert Stephanie Culp is the author of several books, including *How to Conquer Clutter*, *Conquering the Paper Pile-Up*, *Organized Closets & Storage for Every Room in the House*, and *Streamlining Your Life*. Her organization and management consulting firm, The Organization, designs and implements systems and establishes procedures to help businesses and people get, and stay, organized so that they can benefit from maximum personal power and professional productivity.

Culp is a national lecturer and seminar leader specializing in time and paper management. Her articles have appeared in several publications, including *The Los Angeles Times*, *Redbook*, *Working Woman*, *Family Circle*, and *Milwaukee Magazine*.

She was elected as a delegate from Southern California to the White House Conference on Small Business in Washington D.C. in 1986. She is a founding member and the past president of the National Association of Professional Organizers; she has received that association's award for outstanding contribution to the profession three times and is the only professional organizer to hold that distinction.

If you want additional information about
LECTURES OR PERSONAL APPEARANCES BY STEPHANIE CULP
FOR YOUR GROUP OR ORGANIZATION

send your request to: Stephanie Culp
THE ORGANIZATION
P.O. Box 108
Oconomowoc, WI 53066
(414)567-9035